Kim Terakes' twenty-five-year advertising career was really just an excuse to have lunch in restaurants every day. He has since given up the pretence and now devotes himself exclusively to the cause of good food. Since the late 1980s, he has written about food and restaurants for publications such as *Australian Gourmet Traveller*, *Vogue Entertaining*, *BRW*, *SMH Good Living* and the *Sunday Telegraph*. He was the restaurant reviewer for the *Sun Herald* for several years, contributed to the *Good Food Guide* throughout the 1990s and was the food writer for *GQ* magazine for seven years. He currently has a weekly column in the *Sun Herald* and *The Sunday Age*.

Kim started the Boys Can Cook cooking school (boyscancook.com.au) in 2004. He also runs aussiebarbie.com.au, which now has over 25,000 members. His first book, *The Great Aussie Barbie Cookbook* (Penguin, 2007), was one of two winners in the Best Barbecue Book in the World category at the 2008 Gourmand Awards. His second book for Penguin, *The Great Aussie Bloke's Cookbook*, was published in 2008.

The Great Aussie Family Cookbook

Kim Terakes

Photography by
Rob Palmer

VIKING
an imprint of
PENGUIN BOOKS

For Mum and Dad

Circa 1960 in early restaurant reviewer mode

Aunty Jose mid cream fight

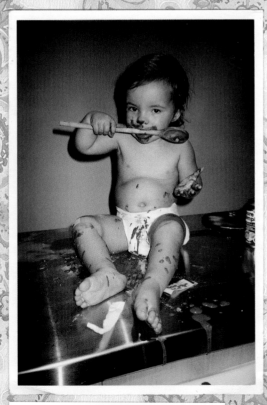

Zoe's first attempt at chocolate cake

INTRODUCTION

EVERY FAMILY IS SPECIAL

When I was growing up, my family was wonderfully ordinary and wonderfully special. So is every family.

Each family has its idiosyncrasies: the characters, expressions and stories that are unique to us. (We had funny aunty Jose, who started cream fights – in the lounge room – when she visited from the country, and Dad's own language that incorporated both fruit-market and racetrack parlance.) Like every family, we were influenced by the combined cultures of our parents (Mum's Anglo-Irish and Dad's Greek), the neighbourhood we grew up in, the school we went to – and the food we ate.

Mum and Dad shared a great sense of family and we ate together at the dining table every night without fail. It was time for all of us to come together, even if it was just for half an hour. Friends were always welcome, too. When I was a teenager, our house was full of my mates and Mum churned out cheesecakes, sausage rolls and biscuits for them. While my parents ate to live rather than lived to eat (unlike their eldest son), the food that they put on the table was a big part of my childhood and has contributed to who I am today.

Because, although we had treats and a little highly fashionable, highly processed rubbish, most of what we ate was real food – fresh meat, some (abominably cooked) fish, and lots of fruit and vegetables. It was a long way from the high-salt, high-sugar and fat-drenched food that has contributed to the obesity epidemic in kids today.

EACH GENERATION HAS A DIFFERENT PERSPECTIVE

In the 1960s, when I was a kid, there were no multi-national fast-food chains, just hamburgers from the milk bar and barbecued chooks. There was Chinese food but no Thai, Vietnamese or Malaysian. 'Serious' restaurant food was largely 'continental' rather than real Italian.

If you were born ten years earlier, just after the war, or ten years later at the end of the sixties, or at the turn of the millennium (like our daughter Zoe), your perspective is entirely different. My Monkees is my daughter's Hannah Montana. Likewise, my once-in-a-while sweet-and-sour pork treat is her all-too-frequent sushi. Zoe would find it hard to believe that there was a time when there weren't Japanese restaurants in almost every suburb, let alone a time that milk in bottles and bread in greaseproof paper were delivered to your door.

Being born in the same year television came to Australia, I tend to look at history through TV shows. My earliest memories are of *Father Knows Best*, where Dad sat at the head of the dinner table and the children were unfailingly obedient. Zoe, on the other hand, has grown up with the magnificently dysfunctional *Malcolm in the Middle*, *Family Guy* and, of course, *The Simpsons*, with Homer scoffing donuts and beer in front of the TV.

Is it any wonder that many of my daughter's generation are overweight and unhealthy if we parents let them live on white bread, chicken nuggets and chips?

It seems to me that our society is quite literally feeding our kids to death. Obesity and diabetes rates are soaring, and the situation is hardly helped by all the computers, Nintendos and Xboxes. Then we parents drive our kids to school instead of walking a few blocks, and fear for them going to the park to kick a ball around.

My environmentally aware, information-savvy Generation-Z daughter will grow up in a century in which it is estimated that one in three American kids will have type-2 diabetes. As parents, we have to come to terms with a changing world, and do all we can to make good food a part of our kids' lives. We need to start early. One of the problems with a processed diet is that it is self-perpetuating: as kids' palates get used to the unsubtle salty-sweet flavours and fatty textures, nothing else will satisfy them.

REAL FOOD, NOT PHONEY FOOD

This is not a 'health-focused' book but a book about real food, with real ingredients, not artificially flavoured, processed rubbish. This is a family cookbook for Australia in the 21ˢᵗ century. It aims to reflect the multicultural country we live in and our access to recipe ideas from around the shrinking globe. It's a book for all sorts of regular families, so there are no truffles, caviar or foie gras to be found. Equally, I have tried to keep the dishes simple. There are no attempts at haute cuisine or restaurant presentations; nothing too cheffy for the family dinner table.

GET THE KIDS INVOLVED

MasterChef has been a phenomenal success. With ingredients and kitchen equipment selling out after being featured on the show, it would seem that more and more of us are willing to try new recipes and techniques at home. However, what is really inspiring is that the show has captured the imagination of so many kids: school-holiday cooking classes are now booked up weeks in advance. There may be hope for the fast-food generation yet …

I hope that you use this book WITH your kids, not just for them. They're more than likely to sit there with headphones in and accompanying blank expressions, eating salty fried crap if you let them. Please don't. Whether they are four or fourteen, get them involved. Encourage them to be adventurous in what they eat. Experiment with foreign dishes from Japan or Morocco or Thailand, and help your kids to understand where the recipes and produce come from. Take them to a restaurant so that they learn to feel at ease in them and get used to trying new dishes. Spend the afternoon making pasta or baking bread or creating pizza toppings. Allow your kids to get their hands on real food rather than sticking something unspeakable in the microwave. This way you will hopefully pass on an appreciation of good food to them so that they can, in turn, pass it on to their own kids.

IN MY DAY

'In my day' is a phrase to drive any child mad. (Even a child who is all grown-up and has their own children.) It was always tougher, harder, better 'in my day'. As the famous *Monty Python* Four Yorkshiremen sketch goes: 'There were a hundred and fifty of us living in t' shoebox in t' middle o' road … and you try and tell the young people of today that … they won't believe you.'

In my day, it was Mum and Dad and my brothers Peter and Damien in a nice house with a backyard on Sydney's North Shore. Technology was an ancient record player and a black-and-white TV with four channels. No pay TV, CDs or DVDs, and certainly no Nintendos or Xboxes.

In my day, the good things were kicking a footy in the yard after school, being able to walk the streets without parents panicking and being one of three, not one of one.

In my day, there was a lot less processed food to tempt us. But we didn't have the range of ethnic cuisines in restaurants, nor access to the extraordinary variety of ingredients, both local and imported, that we do today. You certainly couldn't buy fennel or garam masala or cavolo nero or sushi rice at your local shopping centre.

At the start of each chapter, I share a favourite memory from my childhood, beginning 'In my day …'. These experiences are personal and every one's life is different; no better or worse. I encourage you to take this opportunity to talk about what happened in *your* day. Share your own food memories with your kids, whether they be about cooking with your mum and dad, dishes that seemed particularly unique to your family, or special occasion meals.

They're yours, they're special and they're important.

The Sao* Song

I spent too much of my twenties raucously (read drunkenly) singing along with Pat Drummond in packed pubs on Sydney's North Shore. Pat later turned his back on the pubs to travel around country Australia, meeting people and translating their stories into songs. When I started writing this book, *The Sao Song* was the first thing that sprang to mind. It encapsulates all that was great about my childhood era: coming home from school to Mum's homemade snacks; playing cricket with my brothers in the backyard; the joy of kids just being kids.

When I was a kiddie in the nineteen sixties, each day we'd come home,
Mum'd make us milkshakes and ask how the day'd gone.
Then it was up the back for the cricket match where the whole world came to play
But we'd drop our bats and stop dead in our tracks when one of the kids'd say …

Chorus: Can you put a Sao in your gob in one go?
Can you jam it all in and give us a grin, without breaking the corners off?
Can you put a Sao in your gob in one go?
When I was a kid, if one of us did, that kid'd be the king of the block.

Now mostly Mum'd catch us but she'd fail to see the joke.
She'd say, 'You wouldn't have a brain to begin with. You kids'll bloody choke!'
Then she'd grab the pack and give us a whack and the cricket match went on.
We were backyards full of Bradmans singing 'The Sao Song'.

Chorus

Now it seems all trace of the baby boomer years has slipped away,
Sao biscuits after school and a mum to watch you play.
For the kids are in the daycare centres now from the moment that they're born
And the backyard died of loneliness when the cricket left the lawn.
But in the last few homes where the garden gnomes and the Hills hoist rule the day,
If you listen very carefully you'll sometimes hear them say …

Chorus

Words and Music: Pat Drummond (Control)
* Sao is a registered trademark of Arnott's

IN MY DAY

In my day, it was porridge for breakfast (made from scratch), Rice Bubbles or Coco-Pops (what were you thinking, Mum?).

For lunch, I dined on a white-bread Vegemite sandwich, day in, day out, except for one day a week when I was allowed to buy a Vegemite roll from the tuckshop (back then, we had a lolly counter at the tuckshop too – some kids would spend their lunch money on a hearty meal of Snakes, Redskins and Musk sticks instead of a salad roll). After school, it was either a Monte Carlo from the biscuit tin or, when I was a teenager, some greasy takeaway hot chips or potato scallops wolfed down after footy training, followed by dinner as soon as I walked in the door.

School Days

Weekday breakfasts remind me of those clichéd movie scenes where the world will explode if you don't snip the correct wire on the bomb in 10, 9, 8 . . . seconds. That may sound a bit melodramatic, but trying to get yourselves and your kids fed and ready for the day can be like a battle scene every morning.

'Mum, can I take my Nintendo to school?'
'No.'
'Dad, can I have Tim Tams in my lunch? Sharon has Tim Tams.'
'No.'
'Mum, have you seen my library books?'
'No. Have you cleaned your teeth?'
'Not yet.'
'Mum, Dad made the bathroom smell.'
'Thanks for the bulletin. Why are yesterday's apple and banana still in your bag?'
'Have you seen my leotard? I've got gym this morning.'
'@#&$! Honey, have you seen her leotard?'
'It might be in my car. Hang on; I left my car at the office.'
'@#&$!'

No doubt this scene plays out with your own unique family imprint each morning. The challenge is feeding the little darlings a satisfying brekkie amid the chaos, before packing them off with a healthy lunch that is appealing enough not to be swapped for a couple of Tim Tams at the earliest opportunity. After school is also a good time to get something healthy into them – they're so ravenous they'll eat anything.

START-THE-DAY SMOOTHIES

There's the cordial commercial suggesting their brand of cordial is a great way to get kids to drink water. Or the ice cream or chocolate-making geniuses trying to convince us that their products are the best way to get kids to have milk. It makes me cringe because, really, it couldn't be simpler: a homemade smoothie is nothing but a glass of goodness first thing in the morning.

It just takes a few basic ingredients: fruit, ice cubes, milk and a little honey if needed. Some people like to add yoghurt, and of course you can use low fat if you like. Frozen berries are fine, especially during winter; in fact, frozen fruit produces a better, thicker result than the stuff at room temperature. Washing the blender is the only bummer.

Try these combinations:

- **BANANA AND HONEY (optional teaspoon of cocoa powder or drinking chocolate)**

- **JUST PLAIN STRAWBERRIES**

- **JUST PLAIN MANGO**

- **TROPICAL (pineapple, rockmelon, lime and strawberry)**

- **FIG, HONEY AND CINNAMON**

- **MIXED BERRIES (raspberries, strawberries, blueberries and blackberries)**

WEET-BIX BERRY SAMBOS

Serves 1

This is more about getting the littlies to eat something good for them while having a bit of fun. Save it for summer when berries are affordable, and give them porridge in winter.

2 Weet-Bix, preferably organic
½ cup raspberries, blueberries, blackberries or chopped strawberries
2 tablespoons natural yoghurt (optional)
milk, to serve

Place one Weet-Bix in a flat-bottomed bowl and get your child to arrange some berries on top. Blueberries, being round, roll off so use the yoghurt to hold them in place if you like. Place the other Weet-Bix on top to make a sandwich and squeeze down gently.

Pour some milk over the top and watch the whole thing fall to bits as they try to eat it.

MIXED BERRY HOTCAKES
Serves 4–6 for breakfast

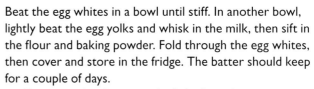

These might sound fiddly for school days, but if you make the batter the night before and use fresh berries in summer when they're at their best and cheapest (use frozen berries when they're not), it's go to whoa in ten minutes. Keeping the batter and berries separate means that you can make just a couple, say for one child, with no waste.

3 organic or free-range eggs, separated
150 ml milk
120 g plain flour
1 heaped teaspoon baking powder
1 cup mixed berries, strained if frozen,
    plus extra for serving
a little butter, for frying

Beat the egg whites in a bowl until stiff. In another bowl, lightly beat the egg yolks and whisk in the milk, then sift in the flour and baking powder. Fold through the egg whites, then cover and store in the fridge. The batter should keep for a couple of days.

If you are planning to cook all the hotcakes at once, stir the berries through the batter now. Heat a little butter in a non-stick frying pan and ladle in about two or three tablespoons of batter per hotcake. Turn when air bubbles start appearing on the top of the batter and briefly cook the other side. Keep the hotcakes warm in a low oven (about 120°C) while you cook the remainder, if you can keep the kids away from them.

Serve with extra berries, yoghurt, maple syrup or even ham or bacon.

Note: If you are only making a couple of hotcakes, ladle the mixture into the pan and immediately sprinkle a few berries on top, rather than mixing them through the batter.

QUICK BREAKFAST OMELETTES
Makes 1

You do have time to whip up a school-day breakfast omelette as long as you keep things simple – save roasting the capsicum for another time. Young kids will probably prefer a slice of 'plastic cheese' – the stuff with virtually no flavour, but it's better that than nothing.

Choose from the following variations and follow the method below. These recipes are for under-tens, but if you are also feeding young teens, simply double the quantities.

HAM AND TOMATO OMELETTE

1 teaspoon butter
1 organic or free-range egg, beaten with
    1 teaspoon cold water
1 tablespoon chopped leg ham
1 tablespoon chopped tomato

CHEESE OMELETTE

1 teaspoon butter
1 organic or free-range egg, beaten with
    1 teaspoon cold water
2 tablespoons grated cheddar cheese or a couple of
    sliced cherry bocconcini or a slice of plastic cheese
    torn in half

CHICKEN AND CORN OMELETTE

1 teaspoon butter
1 organic or free-range egg, beaten with
    1 teaspoon cold water
½ cup shredded leftover chicken meat
1 tablespoon corn kernels, frozen or canned

Heat a small frying pan and add the butter, swirling it around to cover the base. Pour in the beaten egg and cook over medium heat until partially set, then bring the edges to the middle and allow the liquid to run to the sides. Add the filling to one half of the omelette and cook to heat through or melt the cheese. Fold the omelette in half with a spatula and serve immediately.

GIDDY-UP GRILLS ›
Each serves 2–4

Heat up the grill while you throw a couple of easy-to-find ingredients onto slices of bread. Cheese is a mandatory so it can melt all over, warming up the start of your day.

CHEESE AND TOMATO GRILLS

4 slices multigrain bread
about 8 slices ripe tomato
2 slices sandwich cheese (cheddar or Swiss for the big
    kids, 'plastic' for the littlies and maybe hand-cut
    gruyère for you)
freshly ground black pepper (optional)

Grill one side of the bread slices. Turn them over and top with the tomato and then the cheese. Season with a little pepper if you like, then grill until the cheese melts and starts to brown.

TURKEY AND CRANBERRY GRILLS

4 slices multigrain bread
⅓ cup cranberry sauce
1½ cups shredded leftover turkey or chicken meat
4 slices Swiss cheese

Grill one side of the bread slices. Turn them over and spread with cranberry sauce, then top with shredded turkey or chicken and the cheese. Grill until the cheese melts and starts to brown.

AVOCADO CHEESE MELTS

4 slices multigrain bread
1 ripe avocado, sliced
4 slices cheddar cheese

Grill one side of the bread slices. Turn them over and top with the avocado and then the cheese. Grill until the cheese melts and starts to brown.

‹ WRAP IT UP

For some reason a wrap is more interesting than a sandwich for an eight-year-old, which I sort of understand. As with sambos, the number of possible filling combinations is just about endless. Wraps are a great way to use up leftovers like the meatballs from Spaghetti and Meatballs (page 109). My only advice would be to avoid all things runny so the filling won't leak all over their school uniforms. Here's a few ideas to get you started.

CHICKEN

shredded leftover roast chook or some BBQ takeaway (one breast goes a long way)
mayo
green salad leaves (butter lettuce, rocket, watercress – whatever takes your fancy)

BARBECUE

shredded leftover beef brisket
lettuce
BBQ sauce: combine ⅓ cup tomato sauce, 1 teaspoon Worcestershire sauce, 1 teaspoon cider vinegar, ½ teaspoon dried mustard powder and 1 tablespoon brown sugar in a saucepan or in a microwave-proof bowl and cook until the sugar has dissolved. Stir a tablespoon of sauce through one portion of the beef.

VEGGIE

½ avocado, mashed
¼ red capsicum, white insides and seeds removed, finely chopped
2 tablespoons canned corn kernels
1 golden shallot, very finely diced
green salad leaves (optional)

SCHOOL-LUNCH SAMBOS

Try to think the opposite of Vegemite sandwiches on white bread. The giant sambos on pages 84 and 91 in Weekend Lunches might be a bit over the top for the pressure of a school-day morning, but you can still have some fun.

Try the following combinations, all on multigrain bread.

- **canned tuna, mayo and alfalfa sprouts**
- **mortadella, sliced tomato, Swiss cheese and butter lettuce**
- **leg ham, thinly sliced red capsicum and thinly sliced asiago or provolone cheese**
- **cold grilled thinly sliced bacon or pancetta, lettuce, tomato and mayo**
- **boiled egg with a little mayo and chopped chives, lettuce and grated carrot**
- **thinly sliced cheddar cheese, leg ham, chutney and boiled egg**
- **sliced tomato and bocconcini with thinly sliced cheddar cheese**

IN THE SOUP

Serves 6

Vegetable soups are healthy to eat and simple to make – as parents, these words are music to our ears. They're easy to heat up for a Thermos for lunch or for a healthy snack after school. My daughter Zoe loves a combination of onion and potato with lots of carrots and zucchini, and will happily eat it cold from the fridge (yuk) when she gets home from school.

Here are four other faves. Pick one and follow the simple method below.

CARROT

1 leek
4 carrots
½ teaspoon ground coriander

PUMPKIN

1 small onion
500 g pumpkin
½ teaspoon ground cinnamon

GREEN SOUP

1 small onion
1 cup fresh or frozen peas
2 zucchini
1 tablespoon chopped mint

LEEK AND POTATO (LET'S NOT TELL THEM IT'S VICHYSSOISE)

1 leek
500 g potatoes
1 tablespoon chopped chives (optional)
Note: You will need chicken stock to make this one work

The principal is the same for all of them. Chop the veg into even-sized pieces. Heat about a teaspoon of neutral oil (see opposite) in a large saucepan and soften onion or leek, then add the veg and seasoning and cook in enough chicken stock or water to cover. Whack the lot through a food processor or be lazy like me and use a stab blender (add more stock or water if the soup is too thick).

RAW VEGETABLES AND DIPPING SAUCES ›

Things don't get much healthier than raw vegetables. Trust me to match them with some oil-based but yummy dipping sauces to make them more interesting. You want nice firm veggies that will stay that way until lunch time: carrot and celery are the best, followed by capsicum (any colour). Chunks of hard cheese are another good option.

The dips below will all survive half a day in a lunchbox. The vinaigrettes are yummy but perhaps too messy for the under-ten brigade.

SIMPLE TOMATO MAYO DIP

2 tablespoons egg mayonnaise
1 teaspoon tomato paste

CHICKPEA AND MINT DIP

½ cup canned chickpeas, rinsed, drained and mashed
1 tablespoon olive oil, plus extra if needed
½ clove garlic, crushed (optional)
1 tablespoon finely chopped mint

TOMATO AND OLIVE DIP

1 tablespoon black olive tapenade or finely chopped black olives
1 tablespoon finely chopped semi-dried or sun-dried tomatoes
1 tablespoon shredded basil

BALSAMIC VINAIGRETTE DIPPING SAUCE

2 tablespoons extra virgin olive oil
1 tablespoon balsamic vinegar
sea salt and freshly ground black pepper, to taste

ORIENTAL DIPPING SAUCE

2 tablespoons neutral oil (such as vegetable, canola, safflower or mild peanut oil)
1 tablespoon mirin
1 teaspoon sesame oil
1 tablespoon kecap manis

MISO SOUP WITH SNOWPEAS

Serves 1

I feel very old, full stop. But I feel especially old watching my little girl tuck into a bowl of miso soup after school and remembering what I used to eat at that age. Miso is a relatively recent discovery for me, but thanks to my daughter Zoe we've had packets of it in the pantry since she was at kindy.

This is as much a tip as a recipe. To offset my concern about all the chemicals in instant miso, I like to add some raw snowpeas and fresh tofu if there's some in the fridge.

1 individual serve miso soup (it usually comes with a paste and a dried spice package)
3–4 snowpeas, sliced diagonally
1 tablespoon diced silken tofu (optional)

Make up the soup according to the packet instructions (ie, pour a cup of boiling water on the soup base). Add the snowpeas and tofu immediately. The snowpeas will cook a little in the boiling water but should still retain crunch.

KIDS' CRUNCHY SALAD ›

Makes 4 small servings

Crunchy is good; limp is bad when it comes to salads, so pick things that won't fade by lunch time. Whether you dress the salad with the vinaigrette depends on the age and tastes of your kids.

1 stalk celery, thickly sliced
½ red capsicum, white insides and seeds removed, sliced or chopped
½ green capsicum, white insides and seeds removed, sliced or chopped
1 carrot, sliced
½ cup pitted olives
about 12 sugar snap peas, blanched in boiling water for a few seconds, then placed in iced water and drained
½ cup grape or small cherry tomatoes

VINAIGRETTE (OPTIONAL)
2 tablespoons neutral oil (see page 14)
1 tablespoon white-wine vinegar
1 teaspoon honey mustard

Mix together the vinaigrette ingredients. Toss through the salad ingredients or send to school in a separate container.

VEGGIE FRITTATA
Serves 8–12

Once you get the knack of cooking them, frittatas are the sort of dish you can make with literally dozens of variations. You do need the knack though – the trick being to cook them through without burning the bum out of them.

As an old advertising bloke, my motto is: if in doubt, cheat. Purists would never cover the top of the frying pan with a large lid to half fry/half steam the frittata, but do we care? I didn't think so.

1 tablespoon olive oil
40 g butter
1 large brown onion, finely sliced
1 clove garlic, crushed
3 zucchini, sliced or coarsely grated
8 organic or free-range eggs
sea salt and freshly ground black pepper
⅔ cup finely grated parmesan cheese
½ cup roughly chopped flat-leaf parsley

Heat the oil and half the butter in a large frying pan. Add the onion and garlic and cook over medium heat until the onion starts to colour. Add the zucchini and cook over high heat until softened. Remove to a large bowl.

Beat the eggs and season well with salt and pepper. Add the cheese, parsley and the cooked veg, mixing all the time so the eggs don't cook from the heat of the veg.

Melt the remaining butter in a 16–20 cm non-stick frying pan, tilting it to cover the base and sides completely. Add the egg mixture and place a large lid over the top, then cook over the lowest possible heat until the eggs set all the way through. If they refuse, place the pan under a medium grill, watching it every second. Serve warm or cold. This will keep for a couple of days in the fridge.

SOBA NOODLES WITH TOFU ›
Serves 2

The downside of two-minute noodles is that they are full of salt, chemicals and preservatives (says me whose daughter devours miso soup on a regular basis). The upside, of course, is that kids love them. I like to think this version will still appeal to kids, while being much better for them. Make up a batch and store it in the fridge – you should get a couple of days out of it.

200 g soba noodles
1 tablespoon dried wakame (seaweed),
    reconstituted in hot water
2 spring onions, sliced
½ cup diced tofu (either hard or silken)
1 tablespoon sesame seeds
1 tablespoon neutral oil (see page 14)
1 tablespoon light soy
½ teaspoon sesame oil

Cook the noodles following the packet instructions, then drain and place in iced water. Drain again very thoroughly and mix with the remaining ingredients.

SCHOOL-LUNCH S'GETTI

Makes 4 servings

Most kids prefer to eat pasta than just about anything else put in front of them,
so pasta in the lunchbox is a bit of a treat. Leftover spag bol is the most
obvious – penne is less messy to eat, but probably not as much fun.
Try throwing together penne with bocconcini, cherry tomatoes and basil
for a really quick and easy lunchbox solution. Here are a couple
of other pasta ideas.

FUSILLI WITH CAPSICUM, RED ONION AND PANCETTA

1 tablespoon olive oil
2 thin slices pancetta, finely chopped
1 small red onion, thinly sliced
1 small red capsicum, white insides and seeds removed,
    cut into 1 cm pieces
½ small yellow capsicum, white insides and seeds
    removed, cut into 1 cm pieces
1 clove garlic, finely chopped (optional)
1 × 400 g can Italian diced tomatoes
200 g dried fusilli or penne

Heat the oil in a frying pan. Cook the pancetta for a
minute, then add the onion, capsicum and garlic (if using)
and cook until soft but not coloured.

Add the tomato and simmer for 5 minutes. Cook the
pasta in lots of boiling salted water until al dente. Drain.
Add the pasta to the sauce and mix well.

PENNE WITH TOMATO AND VEGETABLE SAUCE

1 tablespoon olive oil
1 small onion, finely sliced
1 clove garlic, finely chopped or crushed (optional)
2 carrots, roughly chopped or sliced
2 zucchini, roughly chopped or sliced
⅔ cup fresh or frozen peas
1 × 400 g can Italian diced tomatoes
2 tablespoons roughly chopped basil or flat-leaf parsley
200 g dried penne

Heat the oil in a frying pan and soften the onion and garlic
(if using) over medium heat without browning. Stir in the
carrot, zucchini and peas until well coated with the oil and
cook for a minute or so. Add the tomato and simmer until
the carrot is soft. Stir in the basil or parsley. Cook the
pasta in lots of boiling salted water until al dente. Drain.
Add the pasta to the sauce and mix well.

NO-FUSS FRIED RICE

Serves 4

The traditional Australian version of fried rice with char siu (Chinese barbecue pork) and prawns is a fine thing, but can be tough for an after-school snack unless you live near a Chinese BBQ shop.

This version doesn't pretend to be authentic, but it will give the kids a filling snack that's not too bad for them either. When cooking rice for fried rice, boil it in plenty of salted water then chill it for a while to stop the grains from sticking together.

2 tablespoons neutral oil (see page 14)
½ chicken breast, very finely sliced
2 spring onions, sliced
1 cup frozen corn kernels
½ cup frozen peas
½ small red capsicum, white insides and seeds removed, diced
3 cups cooked long-grain rice, chilled
2 tablespoons light soy sauce

Heat the oil in a wok and stir-fry the chicken until it changes colour. Add the spring onion, corn, peas and capsicum and cook for a minute or two without allowing the veggies to colour. Add the rice and heat right through, then add the soy sauce and stir to coat completely.

ZOE'S FROZEN TREATS ›

Makes 4–6

Kids love making 'concoctions' for Mum and Dad to try – you know, the whipped cream, gravy, strawberry jam and tomato sauce variety. But as the kids get bigger (and with a bit of subtle direction), these concoctions can become almost palatable.

Zoe invented the first of these frozen treats fair and square (two ingredients only, I know) and had just a bit of help with the second one.

FROZEN STRAWBERRY YOGHURT ICY POLES

1 cup washed ripe strawberries
2 cups natural yoghurt

Place both ingredients in a bowl and roughly purée with a stab blender – a few chunks of strawberry is a good thing. Pour into ice-block moulds and freeze.

CHOC RASPBERRY COCONUT ICY POLES

⅔ cup raspberries (frozen is fine)
450–500 ml coconut milk
1 tablespoon chocolate bits

Put the raspberries and coconut milk in a bowl and roughly purée with a stab blender. Stir in the chocolate bits, then pour into ice-block moulds and freeze.

Making Pizza

Yes, pizzas can be delivered to your door before you've even put the phone down, but they're actually heaps of fun for kids to make and pretty well foolproof. All you need is flour, a little olive oil, some water and one of those little yeast sachets and away you go. Kids love watching the dough rise and usually take the instruction to punch it down literally. (Note: if they're not covered in flour they're not having enough fun.)

Because I take myself way too seriously, I cannot recommend putting pineapple in the same room as a pizza. When it comes to toppings, I believe simple is best: some tomato sauce, a little fresh mozzarella and maybe some prosciutto or a few basil leaves. But kids are kids, and pineapple will probably be the least offensive thing they want to put on them. Here are my tried-and-true recipes for the base and tomato sauce.

Real home-delivered pizza

Makes 1

PIZZA BASE
1 × 7 g sachet dried yeast
¾ cup warm water
2 cups plain flour, plus extra for dusting
2 tablespoons olive oil

SIMPLE TOMATO SAUCE
1 × 400 g can Italian diced tomatoes
1 teaspoon dried oregano
½ teaspoon salt

To make the pizza base, mix the yeast with the warm water and set aside for 10 minutes until it starts to bubble a little.

Combine the flour, olive oil and yeast mixture in a large bowl to make a soft dough. Turn out onto a lightly floured work surface and knead for 10 minutes until smooth. Return the dough to the bowl, cover with plastic film and place somewhere warm for 30 minutes – the dough should double in size.

Turn the dough out onto the work surface and 'punch' it to remove the air inside. Knead for another minute, then rest in the bowl for 10 minutes more to ensure the best result. Preheat the oven to its highest setting.

To make the topping, purée the tomato with a stab blender or in a food processor. Stir in the oregano and salt.

Roll out the dough on a floured surface to your desired thickness (thin is so, so fashionable, but I'm old enough to remember the Chicago-style deep-dish pizza fad). Place on a pizza tray and roll the edges if you like. Spread a little of the tomato sauce over the dough, followed by a few slices of fresh mozzarella and a couple of torn basil leaves. That's for me – they can have the ham and pineapple with plastic cheese.

Bake for 10–15 minutes until the dough turns crisp – it'll take longer if they keep opening the door to see if it is ready.

IN MY DAY

In my day, we had it pretty good – the quality was always terrific, but the range very limited. Steaks: fillet, T-bone or scotch fillet, cooked beyond grey. Lamb chops or cutlets: occasionally crumbed, cooked beyond grey. Roasts: chicken, pork, lamb or beef, cooked beyond grey. And there was spag bol (without garlic – go figure), the occasional moussaka and the one dish that our family had that no one else seemed to: chicken boiled with vegetables, then the stock drained and rice cooked in it to make a risotto of sorts. Despite Dad working at the market, the veg portfolio was made up of potatoes, onions, pumpkin, celery, beans, carrots, peas and (the ringer) chokos – that was it. I was a teenager before I tried avocado, capsicum, leek or even mushrooms. It sounds so narrow in hindsight, but I wonder how many people ate better back then?

Weeknight Survival

	KIM	ZOE	NAOMI
MONDAY			
TUESDAY			
WEDNESDAY			
THURSDAY			
FRIDAY			

In ancient sitcoms, by the time Dad came home from the office (no one worked in a factory in TV-land), Mum had the housework done, the kids bathed and dinner on the table. Just like now, huh?

In fact these days, while Mum might still do the housework, bathe the kids and get dinner on the table, she most likely also works as well, so the weeknight dinner is hardly the whole focus of her being. Plus, Dad is also likely to have a hand in the cooking, although his culinary repertoire might be pretty skinny. Dinner needs to be fast, appetising and at least vaguely healthy, but never dreary or repetitive. You don't need recipes for grilled lamb chops – what you do need are recipes for dishes that are quick and interesting. If you have backed yourself into a corner by serving chicken breasts and variations of fried potatoes every night, the road back may be a long one, but there's no time like the present to get started on it.

PARMESAN, PROSCIUTTO AND SAGE MACARONI

Serves 4

Here's an easy twist on macaroni cheese that takes no more work. I like to make sure some of the prosciutto and sage is sticking out the top so it crisps up as it cooks. This needs some crusty bread and a sharply dressed green salad to cut through the richness of the pasta.

400 g dried macaroni
300 ml pouring cream
300 ml milk
150 g parmesan cheese, finely grated
4 thin slices prosciutto, cut widthways into 1 cm slices
about 16 large sage leaves, torn
sea salt and freshly ground black pepper

Preheat the oven to 220°C.

Cook the macaroni in lots of boiling salted water until al dente.

While the pasta is cooking, place the cream, milk and three-quarters of the cheese in a small saucepan and gently heat to melt the cheese.

Drain the pasta and pour into a baking dish. Add the cream mixture, prosciutto and sage and season with salt and pepper, stirring to incorporate all the ingredients.

Top with the remaining parmesan and bake for 10–15 minutes until the cream is boiling and the parmesan is golden brown.

SPAGHETTI WITH MUSSELS AND TOMATO SAUCE ›

Serves 4

The trick with this is to undercook the pasta slightly the first time around, then let it finish cooking in the sauce, soaking up all the flavours.

I like the Kinkawooka or Boston Bay mussels you can find vacuum-packed in the supermarket.

400 g dried spaghetti
1 tablespoon olive oil
2 cloves garlic, finely chopped
1 onion, very finely chopped
1 small red chilli, seeds removed,
    very finely chopped (optional)
500 g very ripe tomatoes, seeds removed and flesh
    chopped or 1 × 400 g can Italian diced tomatoes
2 kg fresh mussels, beards removed
½ teaspoon finely grated lemon zest
½ cup each of chopped basil and flat-leaf parsley
freshly ground black pepper
extra virgin olive oil, for drizzling (optional)
salad and crusty bread, to serve

Cook the spaghetti in lots of boiling salted water until just al dente, but still quite firm. Drain.

Meanwhile, heat the olive oil in a large saucepan with a lid and soften the garlic, onion and chilli (if using) over medium heat without browning them.

Add the tomato and cook for 5 minutes if using fresh (1 minute if using canned). Drain the mussels and add to the tomato mixture, then cover and wait for the mussels to open – this will only take a few minutes.

Remove the pan from the heat. Transfer half the mussels to a bowl and remove them from their shells. Return the shelled mussels and any juices to the pan. Add the spaghetti, lemon zest, fresh herbs and black pepper and stir gently over low heat for a minute or two.

Divide among four deep bowls, drizzle a little extra virgin olive oil over the top, if you like, and serve with salad and crusty bread.

TOMATO AND BREAD SOUP

Serves 4

I love a simple tomato and bread salad with cubes of day-old Italian bread, ripe tomatoes, basil and lots of olive oil and balsamic vinegar.

This is the soupy version of the same thing, and you can make it in 20 minutes from start to finish. It is blissfully simple the way it is, but can be enhanced with other quintessentially Italian staples such as chopped black olives, sliced Italian sausage or some crispy prosciutto or pancetta.

¼ cup olive oil
2 cloves garlic, crushed or finely chopped
1 small onion or two golden shallots, finely chopped
2 × 400 g cans Italian diced tomatoes
2 cups diced day-old Italian bread, crusts removed
2 cups water or light chicken stock
sea salt and freshly ground black pepper
about 12 basil leaves, torn
⅓ cup extra virgin olive oil

Heat the olive oil in a large saucepan and soften the garlic and onion over medium heat without colouring. Add the tomato, bread, water or stock and 1 teaspoon salt and cook for 15 minutes, stirring occasionally to break up the bread.

Check the seasoning and add more salt if necessary. Ladle the soup into bowls and finish with black pepper, basil leaves and a drizzle of extra virgin olive oil.

PRAWN, WATERCRESS, AVOCADO AND WALNUT SALAD ›

Serves 4

OK, OK, you don't usually do starters on a school night, but there's no cooking involved here – and it's delicious. The flavours are a bit grown up for the real littlies but it's no bad thing to spoil yourself occasionally.

⅓ cup walnut oil
2 tablespoons white-wine vinegar
sea salt and freshly ground black pepper
6 chives, very finely sliced
16 cooked king prawns, peeled
2 cups picked watercress leaves
1 cup walnut halves, preferably straight from the shell
2 avocados, peeled and seeds removed, sliced, diced or
**   left in complete halves**

To make the dressing, mix the oil and vinegar in a bowl and season well with salt and pepper. Stir in the chives.

Arrange the prawns, watercress, walnuts and avocado on four plates and spoon the dressing over the top. (For the quicker but slightly less glamorous version, cut the avocado into bite-sized pieces and place in a bowl with the other salad ingredients. Gently fold through the dressing.)

‹ RISOTTO OF LEEK, PEA AND PANCETTA

Serves 4

Teach your kids to make risotto properly and they've got a great cooking skill for life. If they learn how to make one risotto recipe, they can make a hundred because the basic technique remains the same – only the flavours change.

2 cups shelled green peas
1 tablespoon olive oil
40 g butter
50 g pancetta, finely sliced or chopped
1 leek, white and pale-green parts only,
**   well washed and finely chopped**
½ clove garlic, finely chopped
¾ cup arborio, vialone or carnaroli rice
2 cups best-quality chicken stock
1 teaspoon thyme leaves
2 tablespoons freshly grated parmesan cheese
freshly shaved parmesan cheese, to serve (optional)

Cook half the peas in a minimal amount of water over medium heat until soft, then purée with a stab blender. Set aside.

Heat the oil and half the butter in a saucepan or deep frying pan and cook the pancetta over medium heat until it starts to brown. Add the leek and garlic and cook until soft but not coloured. Add the rice and remaining peas and stir for a minute or so until the peas and rice are well coated with the butter and oil.

Add the pea purée and enough chicken stock to cover the rice completely. Bring to a boil, then reduce the heat and simmer gently, adding the remaining stock in batches (then water if necessary) until the rice is al dente and the dish is soupy. This should take 16–18 minutes.

Turn off the heat and stir in the thyme leaves, grated parmesan and remaining butter.

Serve in four shallow bowls, topped with a little shaved parmesan if you like.

RIGATONI WITH CAPSICUM RAGÙ AND ITALIAN PORK SAUSAGE

Serves 4

You'll need to find some top-quality Italian pork sausages for this recipe. The richness and spice of the sausage is balanced nicely by the sweetness of the capsicums. It's a seriously good (and quick) alternative to spag bol.

about ⅓ cup extra virgin olive oil
2 red capsicums, white insides and
**   seeds removed, cut into 2 cm squares**
1 yellow capsicum, white insides and
**   seeds removed, cut into 2 cm squares**
1 small brown onion, cut into 1 cm squares
1 clove garlic, finely sliced
400 g dried rigatoni or other short pasta
2 Italian pork sausages
1 × 400 g can Italian tomatoes
½ cup sage, parsley or basil leaves, torn
freshly grated parmesan cheese, to serve

Heat 2 tablespoons extra virgin olive oil in a large frying pan and gently sauté the capsicum until nearly soft. Add the onion and garlic and cook until the onion is soft.

Cook the pasta in lots of boiling salted water until al dente. Drain.

While the pasta is cooking, squeeze the meat out of the sausages into small pieces and fry in a little oil over medium heat until golden brown.

Add the sausage and tomato to the capsicum mixture and stir in the fresh herbs. Add the pasta and mix together well. Top with a little extra virgin olive oil and parmesan.

VEAL PYJAMAS
Serves 4

It is one of those quirky food things that veal parmigiana is an institution in Melbourne, whereas it is just another clichéd recipe in Sydney. In fact Sydney's $5–10 pub steak is Melbourne's veal parma. Luckily, kids seem to love it wherever they live. In my version, less is definitely more: I don't want crispy breadcrumbs getting soggy in a watery tomato sauce or the whole thing swamped in a pile of cheap grated cheese.

1 cup plain flour
1 organic or free-range egg
1½ cups packaged breadcrumbs
8 × 6 mm thick veal steaks (600–800 g in total)
1–1½ cups neutral oil (see page 14)
1 × 400 g can Italian diced tomatoes, drained
1 teaspoon dried oregano
sea salt and freshly ground black pepper
8 bocconcini, sliced
a green salad, to serve

Preheat the oven to 240°C. Place the flour on a plate. Beat the egg with a little cold water and transfer to another plate, and place the breadcrumbs on a third plate.

Coat each piece of veal with the flour. Dip both sides in the egg, then coat well with the breadcrumbs.

Heat the oil in a frying pan and, working in batches (probably two), fry the crumbed veal over medium–high heat until golden brown. Drain on paper towel.

Mix together the tomato, oregano, salt and pepper.

Place the veal on a baking tray and spoon a tablespoon of the tomato mixture over each. Top with the sliced bocconcini and bake for 5 minutes until the cheese melts (or under the grill, watching it like a hawk).

Serve with a green salad.

MARSALA CHICKEN ›
Serves 4

Browning chicken well, then frying/poaching/steaming it in liquid in a covered pan is my favourite way to cook chook. Browning caramelises the skin and gives it the flavour boost, while cooking it in a little liquid, half sealed with greaseproof paper, makes it wonderfully tender and moist.

1 free-range or organic chicken, cut into 8 pieces,
   or 8 chicken thighs on the bone
sea salt and freshly ground black pepper
2 tablespoons olive oil
1 brown onion, finely sliced
2 cloves garlic, finely chopped
20 sage leaves, torn
½ cup raisins
½ cup pine nuts
1 cup chicken stock
⅔ cup marsala
50 g butter
roast potatoes and green vegetables
   or a salad, to serve

Season the chicken with salt and pepper. Heat half the oil in a large, deep-sided frying pan with a lid and brown the chicken pieces well on all sides over medium heat. Remove and set aside.

Soften the onion and garlic in the remaining oil. Return the chicken pieces to the pan in a single layer and add the sage, raisins, pine nuts, stock and marsala. Bring to a boil, then reduce to a very gentle simmer and loosely cover with greaseproof paper. Cook for about 30 minutes. Stir in the butter before serving and check the seasoning.

Serve with roast potatoes and green vegetables or a salad.

Arranging not cooking

When young people leave home and are finding their way around a kitchen, a good tip is to seek out great produce that doesn't need any cooking – just arranging. It mightn't provide a balanced diet but it can solve part of the problem while basic cooking skills are being developed.

In the bustle of a family home it is often more a matter of time and convenience. Meat and three veg is a lot more attractive with some ripe tomatoes, buffalo mozzarella, fresh basil and good olive oil served as an entrée. Wrap a slice of prosciutto around a bread stick or drape some over a slice of rockmelon for something retro but still delicious.

A simple bowl of good olives; a can of great anchovies; a few different sorts of salami (now so trendy in Italian restaurants); asparagus blanched in boiling water and refreshed, then topped with a little olive oil and grated parmesan or red-wine vinegar; a simple entrée of stale Italian bread, ripe tomatoes, basil, olive oil and balsamic vinegar . . .

The list goes on as long as you can find great produce.

‹ MERGUEZ LAMB RISSOLES WITH COUSCOUS

Serves 4

These North African taste-explosions are for big kids, not little ones. They're a joy to make on weeknights because they're packed with flavour and they're really quick.

LAMB RISSOLES

600 g minced lamb
2 tablespoons harissa
2 cloves garlic, finely chopped
1½ teaspoons ground cumin
1½ teaspoons fennel seeds, lightly crushed
½ teaspoon ground cinnamon
1½ teaspoons ground coriander
½ teaspoon sea salt
neutral oil (see page 14), for pan-frying
lemon wedges, to serve

COUSCOUS

250 g couscous
1 cup boiling water
2 tablespoons honey
½ cup sultanas, soaked in 2 tablespoons water and
  2 tablespoons white-wine vinegar for 1 hour
½ cup slivered almonds, toasted
½ cup finely chopped red capsicum
1 bunch coriander, leaves picked

To make the couscous, place it in a heatproof bowl. Combine the boiling water and honey and stir through the couscous. Cover and set aside for a few minutes, then fluff up the grains with a fork and set aside to cool. Stir in the remaining ingredients.

  Meanwhile, combine all the ingredients for the rissoles except the oil and shape into 8 patties. Heat the oil in a large frying pan and cook the rissoles over medium heat until golden brown on both sides and cooked through. Serve with the couscous and lemon for squeezing over.

BLUE-EYE, ASPARAGUS AND WHITE MISO STIR-FRY

Serves 4

White miso paste might seem a bit exotic but you can find it in any Japanese supermarket and it adds extraordinary richness and flavour to an otherwise straightforward stir-fry.

2 tablespoons neutral oil (see page 14)
750 g blue-eye or ling fillet, cut into 2 cm pieces
4 spring onions, white and pale-green parts only,
  cut into 2 cm lengths
1 bunch asparagus, woody ends discarded,
  cut into 3 cm lengths
1 clove garlic, crushed
2 tablespoons white miso paste
1 teaspoon sugar
1 teaspoon lemon juice
freshly ground black pepper
steamed rice, to serve

Heat the oil in a large wok or frying pan. Add the fish and gently brown on all sides (do not continually 'stir-fry' or the fish will break up).

  Add the spring onion, asparagus and garlic and cook for 30 seconds. Stir in the miso paste and sugar and simmer until the fish is just cooked through.

  Finish with the lemon juice and a grinding of pepper and serve with steamed rice.

TUNA WITH CITRUS SALSA

Serves 4

Some dishes just seem made for summer. This homemade salsa, with its minty, citrussy flavour, really livens up the fish. You can either cook the tuna on your barbecue or the stove – just don't overcook it (medium is enough).

4 × 200 g tuna steaks (1.5–2 cm thick)
1 tablespoon olive oil
sea salt and freshly ground black pepper

CITRUS SALSA
1 large orange, segmented and cut into small dice
1 small or ½ large grapefruit, segmented and cut into small dice
½ lime, segmented and cut into small dice
1 small avocado, cut into small dice
⅓ red capsicum, cut into small dice
10 mint leaves, finely sliced
1 red chilli, finely chopped (optional)
½ cup extra virgin olive oil
2 handfuls rocket or watercress leaves

Brush the tuna steaks with the olive oil and season well. Pan-fry or chargrill over high heat to medium–rare or medium (depending on how you like it).

Meanwhile, combine all the salsa ingredients except the salad leaves in a bowl and gently fold together.

Divide the salad leaves amongst four plates, top with the tuna and spoon a mound of salsa beside it.

SALMON IN MISO BROTH WITH VEGETABLES ›

Serves 4

You might think it's a bit of a cheat to use packet miso soup, but it's a splendid short cut to tart up a piece of salmon and turn it into a really delicious Japanese dish. Kids seem to love it too.

You can pan-fry the asparagus as described here, or you can give it a quick chargrill, as shown opposite. Take your pick – both are winners.

1 tablespoon neutral oil (see page 14)
20 g butter
4 salmon fillets (about 180 g each), skin on, pin bones removed
1 bunch asparagus, woody ends discarded, halved lengthways
4 shiitake or Swiss brown mushrooms, sliced, plus extra whole mushrooms to garnish (optional)
2 packets best-quality single-serve instant miso soup
1 spring onion, finely sliced (optional)
sea salt and freshly ground black pepper

Heat half the oil and half the butter in a frying pan and add the salmon fillets (skin-side down). Fry over medium heat until just cooked through, turning only once, then remove from the pan and rest for a couple of minutes.

Wipe the pan clean and melt the remaining butter, then add the remaining oil and pan-fry the asparagus and mushrooms (including the whole ones, if using).

Make the miso soup following the packet instructions and divide among four shallow soup bowls.

Arrange the fish in the middle of each bowl and place some asparagus and mushroom around it. Sprinkle spring onion over the vegetables if you like and season the fish with salt and pepper.

Garnish with the whole mushrooms, if using.

HERB-ENCRUSTED CHICKEN SCHNITZEL

Serves 4

You could probably breadcrumb and fry the leg of a chair and kids would eat it – what is it with them and crumbed fried food? Here, the often-bland chicken schnitzel gets a shot of flavour with the addition of fresh herbs.

I cup plain flour
I tablespoon pouring salt
2 organic or free-range eggs
2 cups Japanese breadcrumbs (panko)
I tablespoon finely chopped rosemary
I tablespoon thyme leaves
I tablespoon finely chopped oregano or marjoram
2–3 large chicken breasts, cut into slices less than
   I cm thick
neutral oil (see page 14), for pan-frying

Mix together the flour and salt in a flat bowl. Beat the eggs with a little cold water in another bowl, and combine the panko crumbs and herbs in another.

Coat each piece of chicken with the flour. Dip both sides in the egg, then coat well with the crumb mixture.

Heat a little oil in a frying pan over medium–high heat and cook the schnitzels until golden brown.

Try serving with lemon quarters and potato salad, or with new potatoes and a green salad.

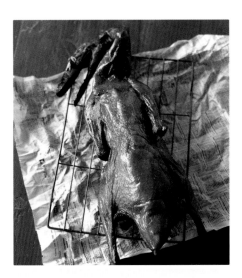

RICE NOODLES WITH ROAST DUCK AND BEAN SHOOTS ›

Serves 4

This recipe works if you have access to a Chinese barbecue restaurant, which seem to be appearing in more and more suburbs in the major cities. If you're not a duck lover or can't face separating the meat and the bones, use sliced char siu (Chinese barbecue pork) instead.

6 fresh or dried shiitake mushrooms, sliced
I small head broccoli, broken into florets
½ roast duck, not cut up by the barbecue restaurant
2 tablespoons neutral oil (see page 14)
2 cloves garlic, crushed or finely sliced
4 spring onions, white and pale-green parts cut into
   2 cm lengths, dark-green bits into I cm slices
about 2 cups bean sprouts
500 g fresh thick rice noodles, or 200 g dried noodles,
   boiled and rinsed
¼ cup hoisin sauce
I tablespoon light soy sauce
I teaspoon sesame oil (optional)
I red chilli, finely sliced (optional)

If using dried shiitake mushrooms, soak them in hot water for 10 minutes to rehydrate before slicing.

Blanch the broccoli in boiling water for 20 seconds, then refresh in iced water. Drain.

Remove the duck meat and skin from the carcass and slice. Discard the carcass and any excess fat.

Heat the oil in a large wok, add the mushrooms, garlic and white and pale-green spring onion and cook for just a minute. Add the bean sprouts and cook for 30 seconds.

Add the duck, broccoli, rice noodles and hoisin and soy sauces, stirring to incorporate and heat through. Finally, add the dark-green spring onion, sesame oil and chilli (if using) and cook for 30 seconds.

RASPBERRY FOOL

Serves 4

Raspberry fool is essentially mushed-up raspberries, sugar and whipped cream. You can use mascarpone and add vanilla beans and all sorts of garnishes if you like, but I think it's best to keep it reasonably simple.

2 × 200 g punnets raspberries
1 tablespoon icing sugar
½ teaspoon grated orange zest
300 ml whipping cream
½ teaspoon vanilla essence
4 mint leaves, very finely sliced
savoiardi (sponge finger) biscuits, to serve

Set aside the best-looking half of the raspberries. Place the rest in a bowl with the icing sugar and orange zest and mash with the back of a fork.

Whip the cream with the vanilla until very firm.

Add the whole raspberries and the mashed berries to the cream and swirl a little, rather than mixing completely. Transfer to small bowls or cocktail glasses and top with a little shredded mint. Serve with savoiardi biscuits.

ETON MESS ›

Serves 4–6

Food is all about fashion, and for some reason this traditional Pommy dessert has become the current darling of restaurant menus – perhaps since chef Andy Bunn put it on the menu at Sopra at Fratelli Fresh in Sydney a couple of years ago.

Fashionable or not, it's a dessert that's easy for school nights, yet not at all out of place at a dinner party with a glass of dessert wine. If you want to make it really quick, buy a small pavlova or a bag of meringues instead of making your own.

2 punnets ripe strawberries, washed, tops removed
1 teaspoon icing sugar
1 tablespoon Cointreau or Grand Marnier
400 ml whipping cream

PAVLOVA
4 organic or free-range egg whites
1 cup caster sugar
1 heaped teaspoon cornflour, sifted
1 teaspoon white vinegar

To make the pavlova, preheat the oven to 150°C and line a baking tray with baking paper. Beat the egg whites with an electric mixer or by hand with a whisk until they are white and glossy. Add the sugar and beat again, then add the cornflour and vinegar and beat for another minute.

Spoon the mixture onto the baking tray. Don't worry about the shape – it's going to be broken up anyway. Bake for about 1 hour until the outside is crisp, then cool in the oven with the door ajar.

Take two-thirds of a punnet of strawberries and purée them with the icing sugar and Cointreau or Grand Marnier. Set aside.

Whip the cream until very firm. Halve or quarter the remaining strawberries and place in a bowl. Roughly break up the pavlova and place in the bowl with the whipped cream and strawberry syrup, and gently fold together. Spoon into individual bowls or serve at the table.

CHOCOLATE AND STRAWBERRY TRIFLE

Serves 6

Trifles are wonderfully simple – just a matter of throwing together lots of store-bought ingredients like sponge cakes, ready-made custard, strawberries and a little booze. This is a bit of a twist on that formula, with lots of chocolate and a nod to tiramisu.

1 punnet strawberries, washed, tops removed, and sliced or quartered
½ cup Cointreau
500 g chocolate cake (homemade or quality ready-made)
4 organic or free-range eggs
125 g icing sugar
2 tablespoons cocoa powder
250 g mascarpone cheese
300 ml pouring cream, whipped
50 g dark chocolate, grated

Soak the strawberries in the Cointreau for 30 minutes.

Break or cut the cake into 2–3 cm pieces and place in a large bowl. Spread the strawberries and Cointreau over the cake.

Separate the eggs into two large bowls. Sift the icing sugar and cocoa into the egg yolks and beat until pale. Fold through the mascarpone until completely combined.

Whisk the egg whites until white and fluffy, then fold through the mascarpone mixture.

Spoon this mixture over the strawberries, then finish with a layer of whipped cream and the grated chocolate.

Super Salads

Salads can be meals in their own right (and I don't mean sticking some grilled chicken in a Caesar salad where it doesn't belong). They also make fantastic entrées or sides.

The joy of salads is that you can use just about anything you like. The key is to focus not only on the quality of your greens and other salad ingredients, but also on the oil, vinegar and mustard – even the salt and pepper – in your dressing. When you are working with just a few fresh ingredients, quality makes all the difference. Make the dressing in the serving bowl, make sure your leaves are washed, dried and cold straight from the fridge, and serve the salad immediately – unlike casseroles, they definitely don't improve with time.

Radicchio salad with fennel and walnuts

Roast beetroot, rocket and goat's cheese salad

Manchego, rocket and pear salad

Frisee, blue cheese, bacon and hazelnut salad

Paris bistro salad

RADICCHIO SALAD WITH FENNEL AND WALNUTS

1 head radicchio, washed and finely sliced
1 small bulb fennel, hard core removed, finely sliced
½ cup roughly chopped flat-leaf parsley
1 cup walnut halves, straight from the shell

DRESSING
⅓ cup walnut oil
2 tablespoons lemon juice
sea salt and freshly ground black pepper

To make the dressing, mix together the oil and lemon juice in a bowl and season with a little salt and pepper.

Gently toss through the salad ingredients.

Pictured on previous page

ROAST BEETROOT, ROCKET AND GOAT'S CHEESE SALAD

6 small beetroot
butter, for roasting
sea salt and freshly ground black pepper
1 big handful of rocket
1 witlof, washed, leaves separated but left whole
½ cup goat's curd
2 tablespoons lightly toasted pine nuts

DRESSING
½ cup extra virgin olive oil
2 tablespoons white-wine vinegar
sea salt and freshly ground black pepper

Preheat the oven to 200°C. Wrap the beetroot individually in foil and add a little butter, salt and pepper to each parcel. Roast for 20–30 minutes (depending on size) until soft, then peel while still warm. Leave whole if you like or cut them in half.

To make the dressing, mix together the oil and vinegar in a bowl and season with a little salt and pepper. Gently toss through the beetroot, rocket and witlof.

Transfer to a small platter and top with teaspoon dollops of goat's curd and a sprinkling of pine nuts.

Pictured on previous page

MANCHEGO, ROCKET AND PEAR SALAD

4 big handfuls baby rocket, washed
I ripe pear, halved lengthways, cored and sliced
200 g Spanish manchego cheese, sliced with a cheese plane
2 thin slices prosciutto, torn

DRESSING
½ cup extra virgin olive oil
2 tablespoons sherry vinegar
sea salt and freshly ground black pepper

To make the dressing, mix together the oil and vinegar in a bowl and season with a little salt and pepper. Gently toss through the rocket and pear slices to coat.

Arrange the rocket and pear on a platter or four individual plates and place the manchego and prosciutto on top. Drizzle with any remaining dressing left in the bowl.

Pictured on previous page

FRISEE, BLUE CHEESE, BACON AND HAZELNUT SALAD

2 thick rashers streaky bacon or pancetta,
    cut into ½ cm pieces
I frisee lettuce, washed and dried, tough outer
    leaves discarded
½ bunch chives, very finely sliced
⅔ cup hazelnuts
150–200 g blue cheese

DRESSING
½ cup hazelnut oil
¼ cup white-wine vinegar
freshly ground black pepper

Fry the bacon or pancetta until slightly crisp and drain on paper towel.

To make the dressing, mix together the oil and vinegar in a bowl and season with a little pepper (it should be salty enough with the bacon and cheese). Gently toss through the lettuce, chives, hazelnuts and bacon. Arrange on four serving plates and crumble the blue cheese over the top.

Pictured on previous page

PARIS BISTRO SALAD

I butter lettuce, washed and dried,
    tough outer leaves discarded
1–2 golden shallots, very finely diced
2 ripe tomatoes, quartered

DRESSING
⅓ cup olive oil
I heaped teaspoon Dijon mustard
2 tablespoons white-wine vinegar
sea salt and freshly ground black pepper

To make the dressing, mix together the oil, mustard and vinegar in a bowl until the mustard dissolves. Season with a little salt and pepper.

Gently toss through the salad ingredients.

Pictured on previous page

IN MY DAY

In my day, Dad usually made ham and tomato omelettes or bacon and eggs for breakfast at the weekend, but every other week, when he worked at the races as a bookie, Mum made him his 'Race Day' brunch: a T-bone steak (cooked grey) with fried onions, a fried egg and a quartered tomato, served with white bread and butter. I don't know why, but it was the best-tasting meal of the week and, despite Mum's protests, I always sat on Dad's lap, wolfing down the salty steak and mopping up the juices with the bread.

Weekend Breakfasts

Remember the days BC (Before Children)? I have vague recollections of decadently spending weekend mornings catching up on sleep, only getting up to play footy or get on the first at Randwick. BC, you could happily spend hours in bed with your beloved, reading the papers (or having a bit of the other – remember that?). You could wander out to fetch freshly baked croissants or cook up something interesting at home for a late brekkie . . .

After Children, weekend breakfasts are an entirely different thing. Although Saturdays and Sundays don't have anything like the crazy pressure of school days, what with sport, birthday parties (they each seem to have three a year), sleepovers and shopping, it's not like you have all morning to plot breakfast.

If you're really busy, do the simple things, like scrambled eggs, really well. Or if you're feeling adventurous, have a crack at something different. It is the weekend after all, and it's not like staying in bed is an alternative.

CRUNCHY GRANOLA SWEET

Serves about 6

OK, it's a dreadful pun with the now very, very old Neil Diamond song, but making your own granola can be fun. The truth is that you can pick any nuts and dried fruit you like as long as you stay reasonably close to the quantities given below.

¼ **cup safflower or vegetable oil**
¾ **cup pure maple syrup**
1 **tablespoon vanilla extract**
1 **cup raw wheat germ**
½ **teaspoon ground cinnamon**
3 **cups rolled oats**
1½ **cups chopped almonds and pecans (walnuts and cashews are also good)**
2 **cups finely chopped dried apple, cranberries and sultanas (dates, figs, pears and apricots are also good)**

Preheat the oven to 220°C. Combine all the ingredients except the dried fruit in a non-stick baking dish and bake on the top shelf of the oven for 25 minutes or until golden brown, stirring every 10 minutes. Stir in the dried fruit and allow to cool.

Serve with yoghurt, milk and fresh or poached fruit.

PROSCIUTTO WITH THREE MELONS ›

Serves 4

There's not a thing wrong with prosciutto and rockmelon as an entrée for dinner or as something unusual for breakfast. But you can have a bit of fun with it by using three sorts of melons and tarting the whole thing up with mint and citrus juice. It's a lovely clean way to start the day.

½ **rockmelon, seeds discarded**
½ **honeydew melon, seeds discarded**
piece of watermelon about the same size as the other melons
2 **tablespoons lemon juice**
2 **tablespoons orange juice**
8 **mint leaves, finely sliced**
8 **paper-thin slices prosciutto, sliced or torn**
freshly ground black pepper

Make balls of each melon with a melon baller. Place in a bowl with the citrus juices and mint and gently mix together. Arrange on four plates or bowls with two slices of prosciutto on each. Finish with a grinding of pepper.

SUMMER BERRY BREKKIE

Serves 4

Forget about this in July when raspberries are $14 a punnet (and not much good). Wait for summer and enjoy this sunny start to the day with no cooking at all.

1 punnet raspberries, plus another 3 punnets
berries (strawberries, raspberries, blueberries
or blackberries)
1 teaspoon caster sugar
2 cups really good yoghurt (King Island honey
and cinnamon works for people like me
who don't much care for yoghurt)
1 cup unsalted pecans, cashews or walnuts

Purée one punnet of raspberries with the sugar. Set aside.
    Wash the remaining berries and divide them evenly among four bowls.
    Top each bowl with the yoghurt, raspberry purée and a spoonful of nuts.

Note: You can use frozen berries for the purée, but not for the rest of it.

COWBOY SANDWICH ›

Makes 1

The name of this just might entice the little blokes to eat breakfast. Get the family in on the act: you can have one person on egg-beating duty, one on the frying pan and one at the toaster.

2 tablespoons neutral oil (see page 14)
¼ brown onion, cut into 2 cm pieces
¼ large green capsicum, white insides and seeds
removed, cut into 2 cm pieces
½ thick slice smoked ham, cut into 2 cm pieces
2 organic or free-range eggs
¼–½ teaspoon Tabasco sauce
sea salt and freshly ground black pepper
2 thick slices white bread
barbecue sauce, to serve (optional)

Heat 1 tablespoon oil in a frying pan and cook the onion, capsicum and ham over medium heat until the onion softens. Remove from the pan and set aside.
    Beat the eggs with the Tabasco, salt and pepper. Toast the bread slices.
    Heat the remaining oil in a small non-stick frying pan. Add the onion mixture to the beaten egg, then pour into the pan and cook until the eggs are just set. Fold in half and serve sandwiched between the toast and with barbecue sauce, if you like.

GINGERBREAD PANCAKES WITH CARAMEL SAUCE AND CRÈME FRAÎCHE

Serves 4–6

Brekkie doesn't get much yummier than this. You're not going to give them caramel sauce for breakfast every week, so slot this one into the 'special treat' category.

2 cups plain flour, sifted

1½ teaspoons baking powder

I teaspoon ground ginger

I teaspoon ground cinnamon

½ teaspoon freshly grated nutmeg

¼ teaspoon ground cloves

3 organic or free-range eggs

½ cup brown sugar

I cup buttermilk

½ cup boiling water

150 g butter, melted, plus

   I teaspoon butter for pan-frying

crème fraîche, to serve

CARAMEL SAUCE

⅔ cup sugar

I tablespoon water

300 ml pouring cream

Combine the flour, baking powder and spices in a bowl. Place the eggs and brown sugar in another bowl and whisk until well combined. Whisk in the buttermilk, then add the dry ingredients and mix well.

Add the boiling water and melted butter to the mixture, and whisk to a smooth batter.

To make the sauce, place the sugar and water in a small saucepan and stir to dissolve the sugar. Cook over high heat until the sugar is golden brown, but not mahogany. Carefully add the cream – the mixture will spit – then reduce the heat and simmer until thickened.

Melt the extra butter in a non-stick frying pan over medium heat, then ladle in a little of the batter and cook on both sides until brown. Repeat with the remaining batter, adding a little more butter if needed.

Place a few pancakes on each plate and top with a spoonful of crème fraîche and some caramel sauce.

‹ PARMESAN AND FRESH HERB FRITTATA ROLL

Makes 1

Here is another omelette-in-bread idea that's as easy as can be. Of course you can serve these on a plate, but kids seem to love sticking them in a fresh bread roll and eating with their hands.

2 tablespoons finely grated parmesan cheese
1 heaped tablespoon freshly chopped mixed herbs
**   (such as basil, parsley, chives and oregano),**
**   plus extra to garnish**
2 organic or free-range eggs, beaten
sea salt and freshly ground black pepper
1 tablespoon neutral oil (see page 14)
1 white bread roll, toasted

Combine all the ingredients except the oil and bread roll in a bowl and mix well.

Heat the oil in a small non-stick frying pan over medium heat and tip in the mixture. Cook until the eggs are just set. Fold in half and serve on the toasted roll with an extra sprinkling of herbs.

SMOKED SALMON, DILL AND CRÈME FRAÎCHE OMELETTE

Serves 4

This is luxurious without breaking the bank. It's also fun if you get the kids involved in an assembly line to put the omelettes together. The trick here is not to cook the salmon but place it in the omelette, fold it over and get it straight to the table.

8 organic or free-range eggs
sea salt and freshly ground black pepper
20 g butter
8 slices smoked salmon
⅓ cup crème fraîche or light sour cream
4 sprigs dill, finely chopped

Beat two eggs at a time and season with a little salt and pepper.

Melt a quarter of the butter over medium heat in a non-stick frying pan and swirl it around to cover the base. Pour in the eggs, allowing them to set partially before pushing the edges to the middle and allowing the liquid to run to the sides.

When the egg is nearly set, place two slices of salmon on one half of the omelette, top with a tablespoon of crème fraîche and scatter over a teaspoon of dill. Fold the omelette in half with a spatula and serve immediately.

Repeat with the remaining ingredients.

BERRY MUFFINS
Makes 6–8

The thing with muffins is that you can add just about anything that takes your fancy: berries, chocolate, apples, bananas – whatever you like in a muffin. We are talking more about a general direction here than a hard and fast recipe. These are best made on weekends when you can share them warm, just out of the oven.

1 organic or free-range egg
¾ cup brown sugar
2 tablespoons honey
2 tablespoons vegetable oil
1 cup milk
200 g mixed berries or just one type (frozen are fine)
2 cups plain flour
2 teaspoons baking powder
1 teaspoon ground cinnamon
2 tablespoons demerara sugar

Preheat the oven to 190°C and line 6–8 regular muffin holes with patty cases.

Combine the egg, sugar, honey and oil in a bowl, then add the milk and berries and mix well.

Sift in the flour, baking powder and cinnamon and gently fold through – don't overmix. Spoon into the patty cases and sprinkle demerara sugar over the top. Bake for 25 minutes or until a skewer inserted in the middle comes out clean.

PIPERADE WITH POACHED EGGS ›
Serves 2 for a big breakfast

Treat the family with this restaurant-style dish. It's only a matter of cooking the capsicums and poaching the eggs in the sauce but it makes for a special start to the weekend.

2 tablespoons olive oil
1 clove garlic, finely diced
1 onion, finely sliced or diced
1 small green capsicum, white insides and
    seeds removed, chopped
1 small red capsicum, white insides and
    seeds removed, chopped
1 × 400 g can Italian tomatoes
1 tablespoon finely chopped basil
1 tablespoon finely chopped flat-leaf parsley
sea salt and freshly ground black pepper
4 organic or free-range eggs
sourdough or other good-quality toast, to serve

Heat the oil in a large frying pan and cook the garlic, onion and capsicum over medium heat until softened. Add the tomato and chopped herbs and simmer for 10 minutes.

Season well with salt and pepper. Make four shallow wells in the mixture and break in the eggs. Simmer until the eggs are just cooked. Divide between two plates and serve immediately.

Alternatively, use two small frying pans and eat directly from these, or transfer the vegetable mixture to individual ovenproof dishes and break eggs into each before baking in a preheated 200°C oven for 10 minutes until cooked.

Serve with sourdough or other good-quality toast.

SCRAMBLED EGGS WITH CORN, CHIVES AND PANCETTA

Serves 4

I'm a bit of a purist when it comes to scrambled eggs, so if you're going to tinker with the classic version, you might as well go all the way. Being a nutcase, I would cook fresh corn and then cut it off the husk. For those who are saner than me (everyone), please feel free to use frozen corn.

2 slices pancetta, cut into 5 mm pieces
8 organic or free-range eggs
150 ml pouring cream
sea salt and freshly ground black pepper
1 cup corn kernels (fresh or frozen)
25 g butter
1 tablespoon finely chopped chives
sourdough or multigrain toast, to serve

Fry the pancetta in a dry non-stick frying pan over medium heat until brown. Drain on paper towel.

Beat the eggs and half the cream with a little salt (not too much – the pancetta is already salty) and pepper, then add the corn and pancetta.

Wipe the frying pan clean. Add the butter and remaining cream and cook over low heat until the butter melts. Turn up the heat and add the egg mixture, stirring gently but constantly until the eggs are nearly set. Watch closely – you don't want to overcook them.

Spoon onto four plates and top with the chives and a little black pepper. Serve with toast.

BAKED TOMATOES WITH EGG, PARMESAN AND PANCETTA ›

Serves 4

You don't need three rashers of bacon each to have a bacon, egg and tomato brekkie. This version has nothing fried and just a little crispy salty pancetta to complement the tomato and googie. It's easy to double the recipe if you are feeding a crowd.

4 large ripe tomatoes
1 tablespoon packaged breadcrumbs
1 tablespoon finely grated parmesan cheese
2 teaspoons very finely chopped flat-leaf parsley
4 organic or free-range eggs
4 thin slices pancetta

Preheat the oven to 220°C and line a baking tray with baking paper.

Cut the tops off the tomatoes and scoop out the insides with a spoon, leaving just a shell. Discard the flesh.

Mix together the breadcrumbs, parmesan and parsley in a small bowl.

Carefully break an egg into each tomato and top with a quarter of the breadcrumb mix. Place on the baking tray and cook for 15 minutes.

When the tomatoes are just about ready, grill the pancetta until crisp. Place the tomatoes on individual plates and top with a slice of pancetta.

FILLET STEAK WITH POACHED EGG AND HOMEMADE TOMATO SALSA
Serves 4

Steak and eggs finds a lighter touch with this version so you get all the flavours but not the volume. It takes just a few minutes to throw the salsa together, and the steaks and eggs can cook at the same time.

1 teaspoon butter
1 tablespoon olive oil
4 × 1 cm thick slices fillet steak
sea salt and freshly ground black pepper
1 tablespoon white vinegar
4 organic or free-range eggs

TOMATO SALSA
1 large very ripe tomato
6–8 basil leaves, finely sliced
1–2 golden shallots, very finely diced
1 tablespoon extra virgin olive oil
1 teaspoon balsamic vinegar
sea salt and freshly ground black pepper

To make the salsa, cut the tomato into quarters and remove the middle section, including the seeds. Cut the remaining flesh into 5 mm dice and mix with the basil, shallots, oil and vinegar. Season with salt and pepper and set aside.

Heat a non-stick frying pan to very hot and add the butter and oil. Season the steaks with a little salt and pepper, then cook quickly on both sides. Remove from the pan and place on four plates.

While the steaks are cooking, bring a deep saucepan of salted water to a boil. Add the white vinegar, then reduce the heat so the water is barely simmering. Break an egg into a cup and gently slide it into the water. Repeat with the remaining eggs. Let them cook for a minute or two until just set, then remove with a slotted spoon.

Place a poached egg on each steak and spoon a little salsa over the top.

CORNCAKES WITH SMOKED SALMON AND AVOCADO SALAD ›
Serves 4

You would never have considered this sort of thing for breakfast a generation ago, and now it's standard on menus in cafés around the country. Again, I would use corn cooked on the cob, but feel free to use frozen instead.

1 avocado, peeled and seed removed,
    flesh cut into 1 cm dice
½ small red onion, very finely diced
½ red capsicum, white insides and seeds removed,
    cut into 1 cm dice
1 small ripe tomato, seeds and core removed,
    flesh cut into 1 cm dice
1 tablespoon marjoram or oregano leaves
2 tablespoons olive oil
1 tablespoon lemon or lime juice
sea salt and freshly ground black pepper
8 slices smoked salmon or ocean trout

CORNCAKES
3 organic or free-range eggs, separated
1 cup milk
120 g plain flour
½ teaspoon pouring salt
1 heaped teaspoon baking powder
25 g butter, melted, plus a little extra for pan-frying
1½ cups corn kernels (fresh or frozen)

To make the salad, combine all the ingredients except the salmon in a bowl and stir gently to combine.

For the corncakes, whisk the egg whites until firm peaks form. Set aside. Beat the egg yolks and add the milk, then sift in the flour, salt and baking powder. Fold in the egg whites, then the melted butter, and finally the corn kernels. Cover and refrigerate until ready to use.

Preheat the oven to 120°C. Melt a little butter in a non-stick frying pan. Ladle a couple of tablespoons of batter per corncake into the pan and cook over medium heat until both sides are golden. Keep them warm in the oven while you cook the rest (you should have about eight).

Place a couple of corncakes on four plates. Place a slice of smoked salmon on each, followed by a spoonful of the salad. Finish with a grinding of black pepper.

‹ SPICY THAI PORK BREAKFAST OMELETTE

Serves 4

You can either face a spicy pork omelette first thing in the morning or you can't. I can.

1 tablespoon neutral oil (see page 14)
400 g lean minced pork
1 clove garlic, grated
2 spring onions, finely sliced
2 tablespoons fish sauce
1 red chilli, finely sliced (optional)
1 teaspoon sugar

OMELETTE
8 organic or free-range eggs
½ teaspoon sea salt
¼ teaspoon white pepper
2 tablespoons cold water
1 tablespoon neutral oil (see page 14)
spring onion, sliced on the diagonal, to serve

To make the filling, heat a wok and fry all the ingredients together over high heat until the pork is cooked through. Set aside.

For the omelette, beat the eggs, salt, pepper and water in a bowl. Heat a non-stick frying pan over medium heat and add the oil. Ladle a quarter of the egg mixture into the pan and allow it to set partially before pushing the edges to the middle and allowing the liquid to run to the sides.

When the omelette is nearly ready, spoon a quarter of the pork mixture (but none of the liquid) onto half of the omelette and fold it over. Repeat with the remaining egg mixture and filling.

THAI-STYLE TAPIOCA

Serves 4–6

This one works very nicely, thank you, as something to wind up a spicy Thai dinner. It also doubles as a very different breakfast or brunch dish.

1 stick lemongrass, split lengthways (optional)
2 kaffir lime leaves (optional)
½ cup small tapioca, rinsed under cold water
400 ml coconut milk
⅓ cup coarsely grated or chopped palm sugar
pinch of salt
1 mango cheek, thinly sliced
pulp of 1 passionfruit
1 tablespoon coconut cream (optional)

Place the lemongrass and kaffir lime leaves (if using) in 1½ cups water in a saucepan and bring to a boil. Add the tapioca and cook over medium heat for 10 minutes. Stir in the coconut milk, palm sugar and salt and simmer very gently for another 5 minutes. Remove the lemongrass and lime leaves and spoon the tapioca into individual serving bowls.

Serve warm or cold topped with the mango slices, passionfruit and a little coconut cream (if using).

Making Bread

There is something so quintessentially human about the ancient tradition of baking bread. We can only wonder what our forebears would make of today's white crustless stuff that's so full of preservatives that it refuses to go stale . . .

The easiest way to make bread is to buy a domestic bread-making appliance. They're cheap, they're effective and they're another bulky gadget that won't fit in your kitchen cupboards. But if you intend to make bread every week, go and buy one as they do produce a consistently good result.

If your family is anything like mine, baking bread is something you do once in a blue moon. The result is likely to be a bit heavier than the bread you buy at the supermarket, but the whole exercise of combining a handful of basic ingredients, kneading, watching the dough rise and then baking is something we find really rewarding. I'm sure you will too once you give it a go.

Breaking Bread

Makes 1 loaf

4 cups unbleached bread flour, plus extra for dusting
1½ teaspoons pouring salt
1 teaspoon sugar
2 × 7 g sachets dried yeast
1¾ cups lukewarm water
butter, for greasing

Combine the dry ingredients in a large bowl and add the lukewarm water. Mix well with your hands, then turn the dough out onto a floured surface and knead for about 10 minutes. Place in a large bowl lightly dusted with flour, cover with a tea towel and leave for about an hour – it should have doubled in size.

Return the dough to the work bench and 'punch' the air out, then knead for another minute or two. Grease a loaf tin with butter and lightly dust it with flour. Shape the dough to fit in the tin and then cover and leave it to rise in the tin for 30 minutes. Preheat the oven to 200°C.

Bake for 20 minutes, then remove the loaf from the tin and return it to the oven for a further 10 minutes to brown the base. Remove and place on a wire rack, then leave to cool for 20 minutes or so (this will also harden the crust).

IN MY DAY

In my day, my brother and I walked five blocks to the cake shop – not the patisserie or the branded pie shop – and each bought a meat pie. Next door to the cake shop was the fruit shop, which sold pretty much the same produce we ate at home. The deli, with no more than a dozen different cold meats or cheeses, was next to the fruit shop, and the ironmonger, which later became a hardware store, was next to the deli. Of course, they all closed down decades ago.

At home, my brother and I would perch cross-legged in front of the black-and-white TV waiting for *Joe the Gadget Man* to finish and *World Championship Wrestling* to start (a trip to the old Sydney stadium to see the wrestling live was the ultimate if infrequent treat). I was a big Tex McKenzie fan and would have none of Mum and Dad's nonsense that TV wrestling was faked.

After wolfing down the pie, I would torture my younger, smaller brother with several of the genius holds of McKenzie or Mark Lewin (the 'sleeper-hold' guy). And after that, I'd get belted for making my brother cry.

Weekend Lunches

Weekend lunches should be fun. There are balls to be thrown and kicked, friends to play with, football to be watched and new clothes to buy, so let's not get too serious about a feed in the middle of the day. Sambos are the easy and obvious way to go, but with the golden arches beckoning the kids, we need to make something more interesting than ordinary sandwiches (and something healthier than highly processed hamburgers).

I reckon weekend lunches are a great time to involve kids of all ages in preparing the food. Saturday and Sunday lunches can almost be a game. A lot of the following dishes are simply good fun to throw together.

‹ JAFFLES

There's something very nostalgic about jaffles. Jaffle irons that you held in a fire were before my time (it's nice to know something was) but every time someone dug one out when I was a kid, the result resembled charcoal. Now you can buy a perfectly good electric one for under fifty bucks. I suppose they're just a flash toasted sambo, but the fact that they're sealed means that you can pack in wet ingredients and soft cheese that would otherwise come running out the sides.

You don't need a recipe for making jaffles (anything goes really), but here are a few of my favourite filling combinations (try sliced fruit loaf for the sweet ones).

- **leg ham and gruyère cheese**
- **leftover spag-bol sauce (see page 118),**
  with or without the pasta
- **sliced bocconcini and corn**
- **cooked bacon and raw egg**
- **leftover beef and beans from Nachos (see page 88)**
- **shredded chicken, ham, tomato paste and**
  grated parmesan
- **sliced prosciutto, cannellini beans,**
  diced tomato and basil
- **ham, pineapple, bocconcini and**
  a pinch of dried oregano
- **ricotta cheese, pine nuts and honey**
- **mascarpone, choc bits and raspberries**
- **dark chocolate, white chocolate and strawberries**
- **banana, sultanas, honey and cinnamon**

QUICK(ISH) CHINESE PORK RIBS

Serves 4

The 'right' way to cook ribs is to marinate them, gently boil or roast them and then fry or grill them to finish.

This one-dish version is less messy and all the cooking is done in the oven. If you want to spice things up for the big kids or grown ups, just add a spoonful of chilli sauce or some very finely chopped chillies.

2 tablespoons grated ginger
2 tablespoons finely chopped garlic
2 tablespoons honey
2 tablespoons Chinese BBQ sauce
2 tablespoons hoisin sauce
2 tablespoons light soy sauce
1.2 kg American-style pork spare ribs,
   cut in half lengthways

Preheat the oven to 150°C and line a large baking dish with baking paper.

Combine all the ingredients except the pork in a bowl. Brush half the mixture over the ribs, then bake for 2 hours, basting occasionally with the remaining mixture.

Increase the oven temperature to its highest setting and baste the ribs again on both sides. Cook for another 20 minutes, watching to make sure they don't burn.

PAGLIA E FIENO
Serves 4

The name of this pasta translates as straw and hay, the colours of the fettuccine. I used to enjoy this dish for lunch when I was a pup in advertising. Dozens of us would pile into an Italian restaurant in Sydney's Crows Nest for huge platters of pasta, then wash it down with bottle after bottle of pinot grigio and chianti (them were the days).

200 g dried plain fettuccine
200 g dried green (spinach) fettuccine
20 g butter
I tablespoon olive oil
2 cloves garlic, crushed
4 thin slices prosciutto, cut crossways into I cm strips
150 g portobello mushrooms, sliced
I teaspoon lemon juice
300 ml thickened cream
½ cup chopped flat-leaf parsley
about 12 basil leaves, shredded
½ cup freshly grated parmesan cheese
sea salt and freshly ground black pepper

Cook the pasta in lots of boiling salted water until al dente.

Meanwhile, heat the butter and oil in a large frying pan over medium heat and cook the garlic and prosciutto for 30 seconds. Add the mushrooms and lemon juice and cook until the mushrooms are soft. Add the cream and bring to a boil, then reduce to a simmer.

Drain the pasta, reserving a spoonful or two of the cooking water, and fold it through the cream sauce. Stir in the parsley, basil and parmesan and season to taste with salt and pepper. Add the reserved cooking water if the sauce is too thick.

CHICKEN AND BREAD SALAD ›
Serves 4

In the time BZ (Before Zoe), Naomi and I ate at San Francisco's famous Zuni Café, where the food is simple but the quality of the produce and attention to detail make it perfect. Here's my version of their famous chicken salad.

I free-range or organic chicken
40 g butter
2 sprigs thyme
sea salt and freshly ground black pepper
100 ml olive oil
2 cloves garlic, finely sliced
I leek, white and pale-green parts only, well washed and finely sliced
2 tablespoons currants or dried cranberries, softened in a little white-wine vinegar and water
¼ cup lightly toasted pine nuts
¼ cup white-wine vinegar
4 cups roughly torn Italian bread, hard crusts removed
big handful of baby cos, frisee or red oak lettuce leaves

Preheat the oven to 220°C. Wash the chicken and pat dry with paper towel. Remove any excess fat from the cavity.

Gently separate the skin from the meat of each breast and push a quarter of the butter and a thyme sprig into each. Melt the remaining butter and rub over the breasts and legs. Place the chicken, breast-side up, in a roasting tin and cook for 20 minutes. Turn it over and cook for a further 20 minutes, then turn it breast-side up again and cook for 10 minutes. The bird should be golden brown and just cooked through – insert a skewer into the thickest part and make sure the juices run clear. Remove the chicken from the oven and cover loosely with foil.

Heat a tablespoon of olive oil in a frying pan, then cook the garlic and leek gently until softened. Transfer to a large bowl and add the currants or cranberries, pine nuts, vinegar and remaining oil.

Pour off the excess fat from the roasting tin, and stir the remaining roasting juices into the bowl. Cut the chicken into large chunks on the bone, and add to the bowl with any juices.

Place the torn bread on a baking tray and toast under a hot grill, turning once, until nicely browned.

Add the bread and the salad leaves to the bowl and gently fold the ingredients together, making sure that most of the bread becomes moist. Taste and add more salt, pepper or vinegar if needed. Serve out at the table.

BLACK-EYED PEA, HAM AND PRAWN SALAD

Serves 4

Something special from South America for Sunday lunch. You'll need to remember to throw the black-eyed peas (also known as black-eyed beans) into a big bowl of water on Saturday so they'll be ready to cook on Sunday.

300 g dried black-eyed peas, soaked
    overnight and drained
1 brown onion, peeled and left whole
4 cloves garlic, peeled and left whole
½ cup lime juice
½ cup extra virgin olive oil
sea salt and freshly ground black pepper
1 red onion, finely chopped
2 stalks celery, sliced
1 small green capsicum, white insides and seeds
    removed, finely chopped
2 corn cobs, cooked, kernels removed
1 large ripe tomato, seeds removed, chopped
1–2 red chillies, finely chopped (optional)
200 g thickly sliced ham, diced
1 kg small–medium-sized cooked king prawns, peeled
½ cup chopped flat-leaf parsley
½ cup chopped coriander
½ cup chopped mint
1 clove garlic, extra, crushed
crusty bread, to serve

Place the black-eyed peas, whole onion and garlic cloves in a large saucepan of boiling water and simmer for about 1¼ hours, until the peas are cooked but still firm. Drain, discarding the onion and garlic, and set aside to cool.

    Combine the lime juice and olive oil with plenty of salt and pepper in a large shallow bowl. Add the cooled peas and remaining ingredients and gently stir to coat with the dressing.

    Serve with crusty bread and a crisp white wine.

MUFFULETTA ›

Serves 4–6

I love the food in New Orleans, from gumbo to etouffee, from Bananas Foster to bread pudding with whisky sauce. Even the sandwiches are special – like the Po boys (see page 91) and yet another classic, the muffuletta, made with a pile of cold meats and an olive salad with pickled vegetables. Traditionally, you make one large roll, chill it for an hour or two then cut it into wedges to serve.

1 large Italian or French round loaf
150 g sliced smoked ham
150 g sliced mild salami
150 g sliced provolone cheese

OLIVE SALAD
2 celery stalks, thinly sliced
⅓ cup stuffed green olives, coarsely chopped
⅓ cup pitted kalamata olives, coarsely chopped
1 clove garlic, crushed
1 cup giardiniera (pickled Italian vegetables)
½ teaspoon dried oregano
2 tablespoons chopped flat-leaf parsley
1 tablespoon olive oil
1 tablespoon red-wine vinegar

Combine all the salad ingredients in a bowl and set aside.

    Cut the bread in half and scoop out some of the doughy centre to create space for the filling. Spread half the olive salad on the bottom, followed by layers of the cold meats and cheese. Finish with the rest of the olive salad.

    Wrap the loaf tightly in plastic film and refrigerate for at least 2 hours.

    Cut into wedges with a large sharp knife and serve.

MUSHROOM AND POTATO TORTILLA
Serves 4

Sitting somewhere between a tortilla and a frittata, this delicious dish makes an easy weekend lunch served with a green salad and crusty bread. It also works perfectly as finger food at a party.

⅓ **cup olive oil**
5–6 portobello mushrooms, sliced
I brown onion, sliced
2 cloves garlic, crushed or thinly sliced
2 kipfler potatoes, peeled and thinly sliced
8 organic or free-range eggs
sea salt and freshly ground black pepper
½ cup freshly grated parmesan cheese
2 tablespoons chopped flat-leaf parsley
4 sprigs thyme, leaves picked
I teaspoon butter

Heat 1 tablespoon olive oil in a frying pan and cook the mushrooms over medium heat until softened. Remove and leave to cool. Heat 2 tablespoons oil in the pan and cook the onion, garlic and potato until the potato softens. Cool slightly.

Beat the eggs and season with salt and pepper. Add the parmesan, parsley, thyme and the potato and onion mixture. Drain any juices from the mushrooms and add them to the mixture.

Heat the butter and remaining oil in a non-stick frying pan, pour in the egg mixture and spread evenly. Cover loosely with foil and cook over low heat until the eggs are cooked through. If the top won't cook, turn the frittata over using a dinner plate (difficult) or place the pan under the grill in your oven, watching it like a hawk.

METRE-LONG STEAK SAMBOS ›
Serves 4

Now, the great Aussie steak sambo is a sacred thing. It must be made with doughy white bread, caramelised barbecued steak (scotch fillet for *moi*) and fried onion, with either tomato or barbecue sauce. It's the footy club version, just using steak that you can bite through.

This version is good fun for kids of all ages, and makes a good-quality steak roll that's enough for four in one serving.

¼ **cup olive oil**
2 large onions, sliced
about 8 thin slices fillet steak
sea salt and freshly ground black pepper
4 or 5 leaves of any green lettuce
3 tomatoes, sliced
I metre-long (or as long as you can get) baguette,
   cut lengthways and buttered
your choice of tomato sauce, barbecue sauce
   and/or mustard, to serve

Heat 2 tablespoons olive oil in a frying pan and cook the onion over medium heat until golden brown.

Brush the meat with the remaining oil and season with a little salt and pepper. Grill, barbecue or fry the meat over high heat, then set aside to rest.

Layer the lettuce, tomato, steak and fried onion in the roll and top with sauce or mustard. Season with more salt and pepper if you like and serve.

FLOATS OR SPIDERS

My old man grew up drinking sarsaparilla, an odd, liquorice-tasting soft drink that's pretty well unknown to today's generation. He used to love making what our family called 'floats', which was soft drink and a scoop of ice cream in a tall glass with a straw – sarsaparilla for him and usually cloyingly sweet Passiona for my brothers and me (today, I think most people call these concoctions 'spiders'). Use any soft drink you like, but don't forget a long-handled spoon – it's vital for scooping out the ice cream from the bottom of the glass.

THICKSHAKES

Of course you can buy these at the golden arches and a million other places but try making your own at home. It's just a matter of blending some flavouring, about two scoops of similar-flavoured ice cream and a cup of milk. Our family fave is made with chocolate syrup and a couple of scoops of cookies-and-cream ice cream.

Drinks

Instead of having endless bottles of cola and sugary reconstituted juices in the fridge, I encourage you to get your kids in the habit of drinking tap water every day and enjoying freshly squeezed fruit juice, then occasionally making 'special' drinks together. Having a blender helps for smoothies and will do for milkshakes, although a milkshake maker is an inexpensive novelty if you have the room to store it.

Like everything else in this book, making drinks is another food-related activity you can enjoy with your kids, rather than delivering food packages to the rumpus room.

SMOOTHIES

We talked earlier about making basic smoothies
(see page 6) – fruit, milk, ice and maybe yoghurt
or a little honey. You can try a few more exotic
ideas as well. Frozen mixed berries, a cup of milk
and half a cup of coconut milk is fun (sieved for
princesses if necessary); and strawberries, mango
and honey is a delicious combination. There's a
pina colada of sorts with fresh pineapple, banana,
coconut milk and milk, or one for the bigger guys
with black coffee, milk, bananas and honey.
Play around with flavours – you'll soon find
one you all love.

MILKSHAKES

Before energy drinks, bottled water, diet drinks,
fortified juice stands and all the other modern
advances in beverages, kids could buy soft drinks in
glass bottles and milkshakes from the milk bar on the
way home from school.

Nothing tasted better than a milkshake, and I loved
watching the theatre of the milk being ladled out of
stainless-steel refrigerated cabinets (never poured out
of a bottle) into a battered metal milkshake container,
followed by a generous squirt of flavouring and a
scoop of vanilla ice cream. It was then whizzed into
a thick freezing treat that made your head feel funny
when you drank it too fast.

My absolute favourite was chocolate malted, made
with chocolate syrup and a big scoop of powdered
malt. All these years later, one sip can still take me
back to nostalgia of a 1960s milk bar.

VIETNAMESE CHICKEN, PRAWN AND BEAN THREAD NOODLE SALAD

Serves 4

Bean thread noodles (also known as cellophane noodles) are as cheap as chips and so easy to cook with – just soak them in very hot water for a minute, then rinse them in cold and you're done. There are so many Vietnamese and Thai salads made with these noodles. Here I've used poached chicken and prawns, but you can add whatever you have handy.

I small skinless chicken breast
100 g bean thread (cellophane) noodles
2 tablespoons fish sauce
2 tablespoons rice vinegar
I tablespoon sugar
2 tablespoons water
8 cooked king prawns, peeled and halved lengthways
¼ Chinese cabbage, finely sliced
4 snowpeas, finely sliced
½ small carrot, cut into fine matchsticks
2 spring onions, very finely sliced
I clove garlic, very finely chopped
½ red chilli, very finely sliced

Poach the chicken in barely simmering water for about 10 minutes until just cooked. Allow to cool, then finely slice or shred.

Soak the noodles in very hot water for about 1 minute until they soften. Rinse under cold water and drain.

Heat the fish sauce, rice vinegar, sugar and water in a small saucepan until the sugar dissolves (do not boil). Allow to cool.

Place the chicken, noodles, dressing and remaining ingredients in a large bowl and toss well. Transfer to a serving platter.

NACHOS WITH BEEF AND BEANS ›

Serves 4

You can spice up this beef mixture with more garlic, spices, chilli powder and Tabasco for grown ups or bigger kids, but it works gangbusters for the younger ones served with nachos, stuck in a jaffle, or rolled up in a wrap and heated in the microwave. It is easy to make a big batch and portion it into individual containers to freeze. You'll need to soak the kidney beans the night before.

¼ cup neutral oil (see page 14)
I clove garlic, chopped
2 red onions, finely chopped
I small red capsicum, white insides and seeds removed, chopped into I cm pieces
500 g lean minced beef or braising beef cut into 5 mm pieces
½ teaspoon ground cumin
½ teaspoon ground oregano
I × 400 g can Italian diced tomatoes
2 tablespoons tomato paste
I cup beef stock (ready-made is fine)
200 g dried red kidney beans, soaked for at least 10 hours in lots of cold water
I packet corn chips (preferably organic)
½ cup grated mild cheddar cheese
mild sweet paprika, to serve (optional)

Heat the oil in a large saucepan and cook the garlic, onion and capsicum over medium heat until softened. Add the beef and cook until it colours, then stir in the cumin, oregano, tomato, tomato paste, stock and drained beans. Add enough water to cover. Bring to a boil, then reduce the heat and simmer very gently, covered, for 2 hours. Check seasoning and add a little more stock if needed.

Spoon the required serving onto a plate and surround it with corn chips. Top with grated cheese, then place in the oven or microwave to melt the cheese. Dust with a sprinkle of mild paprika if you like.

‹ PILE 'EM HIGH SAMBOS

It's tough coming up with recipes for little kids and big kids, because their tastes can be so different. The beauty of these sandwiches is that they can put whatever they like on them (it's also a great way to turn leftovers into a bit of fun). Start with buttered squares of focaccia (about 10–12 cm wide), then pile 'em up and watch the kids make a mess trying to demolish them. Here are a few ideas to get you started.

- **lettuce – red oak, mignonette, rocket, butter or cos (whole leaves are better than shredded)**
- **tomato slices**
- **beetroot slices, drained on paper towel so they don't 'bleed' over everything**
- **thin cucumber slices**
- **boiled eggs, either thinly sliced or chopped and mixed with mayo**
- **thinly sliced or grated carrot**
- **sliced or mashed avocado**
- **very thinly sliced red onion**
- **leftover roast beef, lamb, chicken, turkey, pork or corned beef, thinly sliced**
- **leftover dips or salads such as tabbouleh or hummus**
- **sliced ham, mortadella or salami**
- **prawns**
- **smoked salmon**
- **grilled bacon**
- **sautéed mushrooms**
- **grilled vegetables such as capsicum, zucchini or eggplant**
- **sliced cheese such as Swiss, provolone, asiago, cheddar, gruyère or fresh mozzarella (you can use more than one)**
- **relishes, chutneys, sauces, mayo, onion or chilli jam**
- **sea salt and freshly ground black pepper**

PRAWN PO BOYS

Serves 4

Po boys are daggy but delicious fried seafood rolls from New Orleans. Having eaten my own bodyweight of them during my visits to the very deep south, I can vouch for their yummy-ness. What's not to like about fried crumbed prawns on a white roll with plenty of salt and mayo and a Dixie beer?

1 cup plain flour
sea salt and freshly ground black pepper
1 organic or free-range egg
about 1 cup packaged breadcrumbs
24 green (raw) king prawns, peeled (good-quality frozen prawns are fine for this)
1 cup neutral oil (see page 14)
¼ iceberg lettuce, finely shredded
4 long white bread rolls, buttered
½ cup egg mayonnaise

Mix together the flour, salt and pepper in a flat bowl. Beat the egg with a little cold water in another bowl, and place the breadcrumbs in another.

Coat each prawn with the flour. Dip them in the egg, then coat well with the breadcrumbs. You can do this a few hours ahead if you like and store them in the fridge.

Heat the oil in a heavy-based frying pan and fry the prawns over medium heat until golden and just cooked through. Drain on paper towel and sprinkle with sea salt.

Place some lettuce on the bottom half of each roll and arrange half-a-dozen prawns on top. Dollop plenty of mayo over the prawns and eat immediately, if not sooner.

PULLED PORK AND COLESLAW ROLLS

Serves 4

In the American south they take their pork very seriously. Combine it with a barbecue and it's like a religion. Here, we avoid the nine hours of cooking, smoking blah blah and keep things nice and simple – with delicious results.

2 tablespoons sugar
2 cups cider vinegar
1 teaspoon chilli flakes (optional)
1 tablespoon pouring salt
1 tablespoon dried mustard powder
1 tablespoon sweet paprika
2 kg pork shoulder, bone in
4 hamburger buns, buttered

COLESLAW
¼ cabbage, very finely sliced
1 small carrot, grated
½ red onion, very finely sliced
½ green capsicum, white insides and
    seeds removed, finely sliced
½ cup mayonnaise

Preheat the oven to 170°C. Melt the sugar in the vinegar and add the chilli flakes (if using). Set aside.

Combine the salt, mustard powder and paprika and rub well into the pork. Place on a rack in a roasting tin and cook for 2½ hours, basting every 40 minutes with the vinegar mixture.

To make the coleslaw, combine all the ingredients and keep refrigerated.

Remove the pork from the oven and shred the meat with two forks, discarding any excess fat.

Pile the shredded pork into the hamburger buns, add a little more of the vinegar if you like, then spoon on the coleslaw. Not exactly elegant to eat, but it's only family after all.

HOMEMADE FISH FINGERS WITH MUSHY PEAS ›

Serves 4

You will find that this becomes a family fave overnight – it is well and truly in our regular repertoire at home. The saltiness of crisp fried fish and the sweetness of mushed-up peas is a perfect combination.

1 cup plain flour
1 heaped teaspoon pouring salt
1 organic or free-range egg
2 cups Japanese breadcrumbs (panko)
600 g john dory fillets, cut into 2 cm wide strips
1½ cups neutral oil (see page 14)
lemon or lime wedges, to serve

MUSHY PEAS
300 g frozen peas
4 mint leaves, torn
1 tablespoon white-wine vinegar
sea salt and finely ground black pepper

Mix together the flour and salt in a flat bowl. Beat the egg with a little cold water in another bowl, and place the breadcrumbs in another.

Coat each piece of fish with the flour. Dip both sides in the egg, then coat well with the crumb mixture. Place on a plate scattered with breadcrumbs and refrigerate until ready to cook.

To make the mushy peas, combine the peas and mint in a saucepan of boiling water and cook until the peas are tender. Drain. Add the vinegar and mash well with a potato masher, stab blender or food processor – don't overdo it; you want the peas to be mushy, not puréed. Season well with salt and pepper.

Heat the oil in a frying pan over medium heat and cook the fish until golden brown on both sides.

Divide the fish fingers among four plates and serve with a generous dollop of peas and lemon or lime wedges.

BBQ SPATCHCOCK WITH
MIDDLE EASTERN SPICES AND FREGOLA

Serves 4

There are rubs and there are marinades, but this is a particularly yummy one that is not too spicy for kids, especially if you leave out the cayenne pepper. Fregola is a semolina pasta similar to couscous – if you can't find it, use couscous or a small-sized pasta instead.

4 small spatchcock, or two small chickens,
backbone removed and butterflied
(ask your butcher to do this)
lemon wedges, to serve

MARINADE
grated zest and juice of 1 lime
2 cloves garlic, crushed or grated
2 teaspoons sea salt
½ cup olive oil
1 tablespoon sweet paprika
1 tablespoon ground cumin
1 tablespoon ground coriander
1 teaspoon ground cinnamon
1 teaspoon ground turmeric
1 teaspoon ground cardamom
½ teaspoon cayenne pepper (optional)

FREGOLA SALAD
300 g fregola
1 red chilli, finely diced (optional)
2 tablespoons sliced preserved lemon
½ green capsicum, white insides and seeds removed,
finely diced
1 small red onion, very finely sliced
1 cup shredded mint
1 cup shredded flat-leaf parsley
½ cup extra virgin olive oil
2 tablespoons lemon juice

Wash the spatchcock and pat dry with paper towel.

Mix all marinade ingredients in a small bowl. Cover the birds with the marinade on both sides, pushing a little between the breast meat and skin if possible. Leave to marinate for 30–60 minutes.

Preheat the chargrill of your barbecue to high. Place the birds (skin-side down) on the chargrill, then reduce the heat immediately and close the lid. Cook for 10 minutes, then turn over and cook for another 15 minutes. Insert a skewer into the thickest part – if the juices run clear, they're done. Rest for 5 minutes in a large bowl or baking dish.

Cook the fregola according to the instructions on the packet and drain under cold running water. Mix with the remaining salad ingredients (best not to refrigerate). Serve each bird on some fregola salad with lemon wedges.

THAI FRIED RICE WITH CHICKEN AND PRAWNS

Serves 4

This is much more of a meal than our Australianised Chinese takeaway fried rice. You can vary or delete the chilli depending on the family's tastes – either way, it still has miles of flavour. I usually boil the rice the day before so it has plenty of time to chill.

1 cup jasmine or long-grain rice
⅓ cup neutral oil (see page 14)
1 large skinless chicken breast, cut into 1 cm cubes
⅔ cup pea eggplant (optional)
6 large or 16 small green (raw) prawns, peeled
    (if large, cut each prawn into 4 pieces)
3 spring onions, sliced
2 green chillies, seeds removed, sliced
3 cloves garlic, finely chopped
1 teaspoon shrimp paste
2 organic or free-range eggs, beaten
⅔ cup fresh pineapple, cut into 2 cm pieces
2 snake beans, cut into 3 mm lengths
½ cup fish sauce
½ cup lime juice
sea salt or sugar, to taste
½ cup fried shallots
1 cup coriander leaves
lime wedges, to serve

Add the rice to a saucepan of salted boiling water, then simmer until tender. Drain, rinse under cold water to cool, then place in the fridge to chill.

Heat the oil in a large wok over high heat and cook the chicken and pea eggplant (if using) for 1 minute. Add the prawns, spring onion, chilli, garlic, shrimp paste, egg and pineapple and cook until the prawns colour. Break up the egg and add the rice and beans. Stir until heated through.

Remove the wok from heat and stir in the fish sauce and lime juice. Taste and check the seasoning – it may need more fish sauce or lime, or perhaps some salt or sugar.

Transfer to a large serving bowl or individual bowls and top with the shallots and coriander. Serve with lime wedges.

BANANA SPLIT >

Makes 1

Let's not even pretend that the banana compensates for the sugar overload from everything else in this. It's a trip down memory lane for anyone my age but today's kids enjoy adding their own bits and pieces. Simply split a banana lengthways, scoop in some vanilla or chocolate ice cream (or both) and decorate with any or all of the following.

- **mini marshmallows**
- **whipped cream**
- **chocolate sauce**
- **crushed unsalted nuts**
- **maraschino cherries**
- **chocolate buttons**
- **hundreds and thousands**

MUM'S CHEESECAKE

Serves 8

Here's the recipe that Mum made right through my teens for my hungry mates (though for some reason I've never been crazy about cheesecake). You could add a cup of sultanas soaked in water or booze then drained, but my mates insisted that it was perfect just the way it was.

250 g Nice biscuits
75 g butter, melted
400 g cream cheese
1 cup caster sugar
2 organic or free-range eggs
1 teaspoon vanilla extract
2 teaspoons freshly grated nutmeg
whipped cream, to serve

Preheat the oven to 160°C. Combine the biscuits and butter in a food processor, then press into the base and sides of a 25 cm springform tin, making sure it's not too thick where the base meets the sides.

Cream the cheese and sugar, then add the eggs one at a time. Stir in the vanilla, then spoon into the crust and smooth the surface. Bake for 65 minutes, turning the temperature down if the cake begins to rise.

Allow to cool, then refrigerate overnight. Top with grated nutmeg and serve with lots of whipped cream.

Making Cookies

There are so many cookie and biscuit recipes to choose from. I don't think that it matters which ones you make, as long as you and your children make them together. Flour all over them, and the kitchen, is compulsory. Here are a couple of Zoe's favourites (OK, mine too).

Chocolate-chip cookies

Makes about 24

200 g butter, softened
120 g brown sugar
120 g caster sugar
1 teaspoon vanilla extract
1 organic or free-range egg
350 g plain flour
pinch of salt
1 teaspoon bicarbonate of soda
200 g chocolate bits

Preheat the oven to 180°C and line two baking trays with baking paper.

Beat the butter, sugars and vanilla together until pale yellow. Add the egg and beat until combined.

Sift in the flour, salt and bicarbonate of soda and mix well, then fold in the chocolate.

Roll the mixture into walnut-sized balls and place on the baking trays, flattening them out a little and leaving plenty of room for spreading. Bake for 13–15 minutes until cooked and lightly golden.

Remove from oven and cool slightly on the trays (only for a minute or two), then transfer to a wire rack to cool completely.

Store the cooled cookies in an airtight container.

Oatmeal raisin cookies

Makes about 24

170 g butter, softened
150 g caster sugar
150 g brown sugar
2 teaspoons vanilla extract
2 organic or free-range eggs
150 g plain flour
1 teaspoon baking powder
1 teaspoon ground cinnamon
½ teaspoon freshly grated nutmeg
1 teaspoon pouring salt
250 g rolled oats
160 g raisins

Preheat the oven to 180°C and line two baking trays with baking paper.

Beat the butter, sugars and vanilla together until pale yellow. Add the egg and beat until combined.

Sift in the flour, baking powder, cinnamon, nutmeg and salt and mix well, then fold in the oats and raisins.

Place heaped teaspoons of the mixture on the baking trays, leaving plenty of room for spreading, and bake for 10–12 minutes until cooked and lightly golden.

Remove from oven and cool slightly on the trays (only for a minute or two), then transfer to a wire rack to cool completely.

Store the cooled cookies in an airtight container.

IN MY DAY

In my day, weekend dinners were much the same as those on school nights, except for the Sunday roast. Cooking wasn't something that we did together – it was more a matter of getting it over and done with. During the week Dad headed to bed at 7.30 p.m. as he had to be up between midnight and 4 a.m. the next morning to work at the fruit markets. But on Saturday nights, Dad sat up and watched TV with us and, occasionally, if he'd had a huge win at Randwick, he'd treat us to a Chinese takeaway – or mum to a new outfit.

Weekend Dinners

Entertaining friends and cooking something special for your family are two very different things.

Even if it's a casual affair, there's a sense of occasion to having friends over for dinner. You put flowers on the table, dig out the right tablecloth and napkins, buy the wine to match the food – generally make an effort. It's all about impressing (even if it's only on a subconscious level).

If you have changed the nappies of those you're cooking for, the need to impress somehow isn't the same.

That said, weekend dinners can give you the opportunity to try something out of the ordinary and show off to your family. You have enough time to shop for more exotic ingredients than may usually reside in your pantry and the space to figure out what to do with them. Try my suggestions on the following pages.

GOAT'S CHEESE PIES
WITH MESCLUN SALAD
Serves 4 as an entrée

These may seem posh but they're really no more than a sheet of puff pastry wrapped around a piece of goat's cheese (although you should buy the best goat's cheese you can afford for this). You'll need the sharply dressed salad to cut through the richness. This is definitely something to share with other grown-ups.

1 sheet frozen puff pastry, thawed
8 cm log best-quality goat's cheese, cut into four rounds
8 sprigs thyme, leaves picked
1 organic or free-range egg, beaten
2 tablespoons extra virgin olive oil
2 tablespoons white-wine vinegar
sea salt and freshly ground black pepper
2 handfuls mesclun salad, washed and dried

Preheat the oven to 220°C and lightly grease a baking tray.

Cut the pastry into four equal squares, then trim away the corners to form four rough circles. Place a piece of cheese in the middle of each and top with the thyme leaves. Fold up the pastry to nearly encase the cheese, crimping it a little to make it hold together.

Beat the egg with a little cold water. Lightly brush the pastry with the egg wash. Place the pies on the baking tray and bake for 10–15 minutes until the pastry begins to brown.

Combine the oil, vinegar, salt and pepper in a bowl and toss through the salad leaves.

Place the pies on flat serving dishes and serve with the salad leaves.

SALMON, DILL AND VEGETABLES BAKED IN PARCHMENT
Serves 4

This sounds tricky but it isn't at all. You're really just steaming the fish, herbs and vegetables in an airtight parcel, then releasing all the fabulous aromas at the table. Plenty of foodie theatre for the kids to enjoy. You could use ocean trout or any firm-fleshed white fish fillets for this and replace the vegetables with very thinly sliced fennel.

4 salmon fillets (180–200 g each), skin on,
    pin bones removed
6 baby zucchini, halved lengthways
4 baby carrots, quartered lengthways
6 thick asparagus spears, woody ends discarded,
    halved lengthways
6 ripe cherry tomatoes, halved
2 tablespoons finely chopped dill
⅔ cup fish or chicken stock
sea salt and freshly ground black pepper

Preheat the oven to 200°C. Line four small bowls with a sheet of baking paper (the bowls need to be a little wider than the fish fillets, and the paper should extend well over the sides). Add a piece of fish to each lined bowl, then divide the remaining ingredients evenly among the parcels and season with salt and pepper. Close each parcel by tying the tops with kitchen twine, then remove from their bowls and place in a large baking dish.

Bake for 10 minutes, then remove from the oven and rest for 5 minutes. Place each parcel in a shallow bowl and take to the table. Cut the top off each parcel with kitchen scissors (with as much drama and flourish as you can muster) and eat straight out of the paper.

FAST AND SLOW LAMB ›
Serves 4

I love slow-braised lamb, falling-off-the-bone tender with the density of flavour that only slow cooking can bring in a very different way. I also love lamb racks cooked quickly and simply, then rested until tender. Here we have the best of both.

I lamb shoulder (about 1.3 kg)
sea salt and freshly ground black pepper
½ cup olive oil
4 cloves garlic, finely chopped
4 golden shallots, finely chopped
I cup white wine
I cup chicken stock
16 sprigs thyme
I rack of lamb (8 cutlets), trimmed of fat
I cup shelled green peas
I carrot, cut into 5 mm dice
4 sprigs thyme, extra
mashed potato, to serve

Preheat the oven to 160°C. Season the lamb shoulder well with salt. Heat half the oil in a large flameproof casserole dish with a lid and brown the lamb on all sides. Remove the lamb, discarding any burnt oil.

Heat another 2 tablespoons oil in the dish and soften the garlic and shallot without letting it colour. Add the wine, stock, leaves from 10 thyme sprigs, lamb shoulder and any juices. Cover the lamb with water and bring to a boil, then transfer to the oven and bake for 3 hours. Check occasionally and skim any fat from the top.

Remove lamb from the dish and shred the meat with two forks, discarding any fat, gristle and bones. Return the meat to the dish and simmer until the sauce reduces and thickens.

Increase the oven temperature to 200°C. Rub the lamb rack with the remaining oil and season well with salt and pepper. Place in a roasting tin and cook for 10–15 minutes or until medium–rare. Remove from the oven, cover loosely with foil and rest for 10 minutes.

While the rack is resting, add the peas and carrot to the shoulder mixture and simmer until tender. Stir in the remaining thyme leaves.

Carve the rack into cutlets. Place a spoonful of the shoulder mixture in the centre of four plates. Arrange two cutlets on top and garnish with a thyme sprig. Serve with creamy, buttery mash.

SPAGHETTI AND MEATBALLS

Serves 4

Warning: do not stand between children and this dish. Here, the meatballs are lightened with egg and breadcrumbs. I say this serves four, but really there will be leftovers for days.

1–1½ cups neutral oil (see page 14)
400 g dried spaghetti
freshly grated parmesan cheese, to serve

MEATBALLS
500 g lean minced pork
500 g lean minced veal
3 organic or free-range eggs
1 cup Japanese breadcrumbs (panko)
1 teaspoon very finely grated lemon zest
2 cloves garlic, grated or crushed
1 teaspoon sea salt
2 tablespoons very finely chopped flat-leaf parsley

TOMATO SAUCE
2 tablespoons olive oil
2 cloves garlic, finely chopped
½ brown onion, very finely chopped
500 ml Italian tomato passata
20 basil leaves, shredded or torn
sea salt and freshly ground black pepper

To make the meatballs, place all the ingredients in a large bowl, working the mixture very well with your hands to combine the flavours completely.

Roll the mixture into meatballs somewhere between the size of a 10 and 20 cent piece. Heat the oil in a large heavy-based frying pan and cook the meatballs in batches over medium heat, turning them once. Drain on paper towel.

Cook the spaghetti in lots of boiling salted water until al dente.

While the pasta is cooking, make the tomato sauce. Wipe the pan the meatballs were cooked in, then heat the oil and cook the garlic and onion over medium heat until soft. Add the tomato passata and simmer for 5 minutes. Stir in the basil and season with salt and pepper as required.

Add the meatballs to the tomato sauce and warm through over very low heat. Drain the spaghetti and stir the pasta through the sauce, then serve with parmesan.

PAN-FRIED FISH WITH SPANISH-STYLE BRAISED VEGETABLES

Serves 4

There are three elements to this recipe. First the tapenade, which at a pinch you can buy, but it is always more interesting when you make it fresh. The pan-fried fish is straightforward enough – just don't overcook it. The real interest comes from the smoked paprika, which works magically with the sweet fish fillets and the vegetables.

½ cup olive oil
1 large red onion, thinly sliced
1 clove garlic, finely chopped
1 large or 2 small zucchini, thinly sliced
1 large red capsicum, white insides
     and seeds removed, very thinly sliced
1 yellow capsicum, white insides
     and seeds removed, very thinly sliced
3 ripe roma tomatoes, seeds removed, thinly sliced
1 heaped teaspoon smoked paprika
1 tablespoon sugar
1 tablespoon sherry or red-wine vinegar
½ cup chopped flat-leaf parsley
4 white fish fillets (150–200 g each),
     such as blue-eye, snapper or john dory
lemon wedges, to serve (optional)

TAPENADE
½ cup pitted black olives
2 cloves garlic, crushed
3 anchovy fillets
10 basil leaves
2–3 tablespoons olive oil

Heat ⅓ cup of the oil in a large frying pan and cook the onion and garlic until soft. Add the vegetables and paprika and cook over low heat until soft. Stir in the sugar, vinegar and parsley and cook until the sugar dissolves.

To make the tapenade, process the olives, garlic, anchovies and basil in a food processor or with a stab blender, then stir in the oil to make a thick paste.

Heat a frying pan to hot, add the remaining oil and fry the fish skin-side down first until just cooked, turning once.

Place a spoonful of the vegetables in the middle of four plates and top with a fish fillet and a dollop of the tapenade. Serve with lemon wedges if you like.

CELERIAC SOUP WITH PAN-FRIED SEAFOOD
Serves 4

Root vegetable soups are easy to make, cheap as chips and always delicious. Celeriac is an ugly-looking bulb related to celery, but it has a milder flavour. The pan-fried seafood is optional but it makes the soup much more special, and the flavours all work happily together.

2 teaspoons butter
2 teaspoons neutral oil (see page 14)
1 small clove garlic, chopped
1 golden shallot or ½ small brown onion, chopped
1 large bulb celeriac, peeled and roughly chopped
1 cup good-quality chicken stock
½ cup pouring cream
1 small john dory fillet, trimmed and cut into 4 pieces
4 green (raw) king prawns, peeled
4 scallops, any hard sinew removed
sea salt and freshly ground black pepper
4 sprigs thyme, leaves picked

Heat half the butter and half the oil in a large saucepan over medium heat and cook the garlic and shallot or onion until soft but not coloured. Add the celeriac, then cover with the stock and 1 cup water. Bring to a boil, then reduce the heat and simmer, covered, for about 15 minutes until the vegetables are soft. Purée with a stab blender or in a food processor and force through a sieve if you like a really smooth soup. Add the cream and reheat without boiling.

Heat the remaining oil and butter in a non-stick frying pan over high heat. Cook the fish pieces and prawns until just cooked through. Remove to a warm plate, then cook the scallops for 30 seconds only on each side. Remove.

Taste the soup and adjust the seasoning, then ladle into bowls. Divide the seafood among the bowls and sprinkle with a few thyme leaves and some freshly ground pepper.

MUQUECA ›
Serves 4

The basics of this Brazilian dish are really straightforward: marinate seafood in lime juice and salt, stew down some veg, then in with the seafood and coconut milk. Dende oil, a highly saturated palm oil used in Brazilian cooking, can be added at the end if you want extra richness (and you have private health insurance).

600 g ling or blue-eye fillets, cut into 3–4 cm pieces
600 g green (raw) king prawns, peeled and deveined, tails intact
½ cup lime juice
1 teaspoon sea salt
2 tablespoons neutral oil (see page 14)
2 cloves garlic, sliced
1 large onion, finely chopped
1 green capsicum, white insides and seeds removed, chopped
1 red capsicum, white insides and seeds removed, chopped
1 red chilli, finely chopped
4 large ripe tomatoes, seeds removed, finely chopped or 2 × 400 g can Italian diced tomatoes
600 ml coconut milk
½ cup roughly chopped coriander
steamed rice, to serve

Mix together the fish, prawns, lime juice and salt in a non-metallic bowl. Cover and marinate in the fridge for about 30 minutes.

Meanwhile, heat the oil in a large, heavy-based saucepan and cook the onion and garlic until soft but not browned. Add the capsicum, chilli and tomato and cook for about 20 minutes until the liquid has reduced.

Add the fish, prawns and any marinading liquid, and the coconut milk, and bring to a boil. Reduce the heat and simmer gently for a few minutes until the seafood is just cooked through. Garnish with coriander leaves and serve with steamed rice.

ROAST PORK BELLY
WITH FENNEL SEEDS AND GARLIC

Serves 4

This is one of my favourite recipes from the past couple of years. The flavours are so gutsy, and the pork needs nothing more than the rocket and lemon to cut through its fabulous richness; include some roast spuds for the boys, if you must.

1 heaped tablespoon fennel seeds

4 cloves garlic, sliced

1 teaspoon sea salt

½ cup olive oil

1 kg lean pork belly

1 tablespoon neutral oil (see page 14)

2 teaspoons pouring salt

rocket salad, to serve

lemon wedges, to serve

roast potatoes, to serve (optional)

Half crush the fennel seeds with a mortar and pestle and add the garlic and sea salt to make a thick paste. Add the olive oil to thin down the paste.

Score the skin of the pork at 1 cm intervals on the diagonal, then make deeper incisions down through the skin and fat just into the meat to portion the belly into serving pieces.

Rub a little of the garlic and fennel mixture into the deeper incisions and the rest all over the surface of the meat. Place in a plastic bag or a bowl covered with plastic film and marinate in the fridge for 4–12 hours.

Bring the meat back to room temperature. Preheat the oven to 220°C. Rub the neutral oil over the skin and work the pouring salt into the scores. Force any excess marinade into the deep incisions. Place the pork in a non-stick roasting tin, preferably on a rack, and bake for 10 minutes. Reduce the heat to 150°C and cook for 1½ hours, checking regularly so the skin doesn't burn. If it starts to, cover it with foil and reduce the temperature to 120°C.

If the skin hasn't turned to crackling, try putting it under the grill in your oven, but be careful – it can burn in a flash. Cut right through the deep incisions made previously so the crackling doesn't crumble. Rest the meat for 5 minutes before serving with rocket and lemon wedges and, if you like, diced potato roasted in olive oil.

Investment cooking – using the weekend to make meals for the week

We all know what a bunfight school nights can be, and the term 'survival food' is becoming very well worn. So it's a great idea to use a little spare time on the weekend to cook for school nights – a little investment in the future, if you like.

I have never been much of a fan of freezing things other than stocks and maybe some bolognese sauce for Zoe, but I do think some dishes work better than others if made in advance. Casseroles actually improve with a couple of days in the fridge (not freezer) as the flavours seem to come together and intensify. Cooking casseroles on the weekend has the added bonus of allowing you to slow cook, meaning you can use the cheaper cuts of meat best suited to simmering for a few hours.

Rich meat sauce for pasta

Four-hour Italian beef casserole
with watercress salad

FOUR-HOUR ITALIAN BEEF CASSEROLE WITH WATERCRESS SALAD

Serves 4

800 g chuck, topside or other stewing steak,
    cut into 2 cm cubes
1 tablespoon plain flour
⅓ cup olive oil
150 g pancetta, chopped
2 large red onions, cut into 2 cm pieces
1 clove garlic, finely chopped
2 cups white wine
1 cup tomato passata
1 tablespoon chopped rosemary
1 large piece orange zest
sea salt and freshly ground black pepper
crusty bread, to serve

WATERCRESS SALAD
2 tablespoons olive oil
2 tablespoons lemon juice
sea salt and freshly ground black pepper
3 cups picked watercress leaves, washed
½ small red onion, finely sliced
1 orange, peeled and segmented

Preheat the oven to 150°C. Place the meat in a large plastic bag with the flour and shake to coat. Heat half the oil in a non-stick frying pan and brown the beef very well.

Heat the remaining oil in a heavy-based casserole dish and fry the pancetta until it starts to brown. Add the onion and garlic and cook until soft, then stir in beef, wine, tomato passata, rosemary and zest. Add just enough water to cover and season well with salt and pepper.

Bring to a boil on the stovetop, then cover and transfer to the oven. Bake for 4 hours, checking occasionally that it's not drying out (add a little more water if you're worried).

To make the salad, mix the oil and lemon juice with a little salt and pepper and toss through the watercress, onion and orange. Serve the casserole with the salad and some crusty bread.

Pictured on previous page

RICH MEAT SAUCE FOR PASTA

Serves 4 with leftovers

1 kg topside, chuck or blade steak, cut into 1 cm cubes
⅓ cup plain flour
sea salt and freshly ground black pepper
⅓ cup olive oil
1 large onion, finely chopped
2 cloves garlic, finely sliced
2 carrots, chopped
2 stalks celery, sliced
2 × 400 g cans Italian diced tomatoes
1 piece orange zest
2 tablespoons chopped flat-leaf parsley,
    plus extra to garnish
1 tablespoon chopped rosemary
1 tablespoon tomato paste
1 cup dry white wine

Place the meat in a large plastic bag with the flour and a teaspoon of salt and shake to coat the meat. Heat half the oil in a non-stick frying pan and brown the meat over medium heat.

Heat the remaining oil in a large casserole dish and soften the onion, garlic, carrot and celery. Add the meat and all the remaining ingredients. Pour in enough water to just cover and season with salt and pepper.

Bring to a boil, then reduce to the gentlest simmer and cook, covered, for 1½–2 hours (you could also do this in a preheated 160°C oven). Garnish with finely chopped parsley and serve with whatever you like. It's great with pasta, polenta or risotto milanese.

Pictured on previous page

IRISH STEW
Serves 4

8 short loin lamb chops
2 onions, roughly chopped
1 clove garlic, finely sliced
2 large carrots, cut into 1 cm chunks
6 kipfler potatoes, peeled and halved
2 sprigs rosemary
½ cup barley
sea salt and freshly ground black pepper

Preheat the oven to 170°C. Brown the lamb well in a small casserole dish over medium heat (you don't need any oil for this – there is enough fat on the chops). Remove from the dish and set aside.

Add the onion and garlic and cook for just a minute until they start to colour slightly, then return the meat and any juices to the dish, along with the carrot, potato, rosemary and barley. Season with plenty of salt and pepper. Pour in enough water to cover and bring to a boil. Cover and transfer to the oven and cook for 2 hours.

EASY LAMB CURRY
Serves 4

2 tablespoons neutral oil (see page 14)
2 large onions, sliced
4 cloves garlic, sliced
1 tablespoon grated ginger
1 tablespoon ground cumin
1 tablespoon ground coriander
1 teaspoon ground turmeric
2 teaspoons garam masala
1 tablespoon sea salt
1 teaspoon ground chilli (optional)
1 leg of lamb (1.5–2 kg) trimmed of fat,
    cut into 4 cm chunks
½ cup chopped coriander
2 tablespoons lime juice
steamed rice, to serve

Heat the oil in a large heavy-based saucepan and cook the onion, garlic and ginger over medium heat until soft but not brown. Stir in the cumin, coriander, turmeric, garam masala, salt and chilli (if using), then add the meat and 4 cups water. Bring to a boil, then reduce the heat and simmer very gently for 2–3 hours.

Just before serving, stir in the coriander and lime juice. Serve with steamed rice.

ROAST LAMB SHOULDER WITH 'SWEET AND SOUR' VEGETABLES

Serves 4

Some dishes have winter written all over them and this is one of them. The 'sweet and sour' doesn't refer to the shiny red Chinese takeaway stuff – here it is as simple as sweet carrots paired with bitter treviso or radicchio, with some earthy parsnips and garlic thrown in for good measure.

I lamb shoulder (about 1.3 kg), trimmed of fat
I tablespoon olive oil
sea salt and freshly ground black pepper
I bunch thyme
2 tablespoons white wine
40 g butter
4 large carrots, halved lengthways
4 parsnips, halved lengthways
I head garlic, cloves removed and peeled
2 heads treviso or radicchio, washed thoroughly
    and halved lengthways
½ cup chicken stock or water

Preheat the oven to 180°C. Brush the lamb with the olive oil and season well with salt and pepper. Line a roasting tin with all but six of the thyme sprigs (reserve these for later), place the lamb on top and bake in the bottom half of the oven for 2 hours. Transfer lamb to a chopping board, cover loosely with foil and rest for 10 minutes. Discard the thyme but reserve any juices left in the dish. Splash in the white wine and simmer over low heat, scraping up all the yummy flavours stuck to the bottom of the pan.

   Meanwhile, half an hour into the lamb cooking time, melt the butter over medium heat in a flameproof dish on the stovetop. Add the carrot, parsnip and garlic and stir to coat, then season well with salt and pepper. Scatter the leaves from the reserved thyme sprigs over the top and bake in the top half of the oven for 45–50 minutes. Add the treviso or radicchio and stock or water and cook for a further 30 minutes.

   Slice the lamb and serve with the vegetables, spooning the deglazed cooking juices over the meat.

POACHED CHICKEN, SOBA NOODLES, EDAMAME AND SESAME-SEED SALAD ›

Serves 4 as a light meal or 4–6 as an entrée

OK, this won't satisfy a 16-year-old boy's appetite after footy on Saturday (grill half a kilo of steak and push it through the door of his room – he can have this as an entrée), but it should keep everyone else happy. It's light and delicious with a lovely contrast of flavours and textures.

400 g chicken breast fillet, skin removed
2 tablespoons sake or mirin
100 g soba noodles
iced water
100 g edamame (soy beans), available frozen
    from Japanese supermarkets
¼ cup mirin
I tablespoon light soy sauce
I teaspoon sesame oil
2 spring onions, white and pale-green parts only,
    finely sliced on the diagonal
2 cups tatsoi or watercress leaves, washed and dried
I teaspoon white sesame seeds
I teaspoon black sesame seeds (optional)

Poach the chicken breast in barely simmering water with the sake or mirin until just cooked. Allow to cool, then shred with two forks or finely slice. Set aside.

   Cook the noodles following the packet instructions. Drain, then plunge into iced water to halt the cooking and drain again.

   Boil the edamame, then drain and peel – you should have about ¾ cup beans.

   Make a dressing in a large bowl by combining the mirin, soy sauce and sesame oil. Add the chicken, noodles, edamame, spring onion and tatsoi or watercress.

   Swirl neat piles around a large fork and place in four bowls or shallow dishes. Sprinkle the sesame seeds over the top and serve with chopsticks. If you like, make extra dressing to offer as dipping sauce.

‹ LOUISIANA SEAFOOD GUMBO
Serves 4

The word 'gumbo' comes from an African name for okra, the vegetable found in nearly all gumbo recipes. They're usually made with seafood, but can also contain smoked pork sausage or poultry. Gumbos should always be rich, but never over-spiced.

½ **cup vegetable oil**
½ **cup plain flour**
2 **cloves garlic, crushed**
1 **large onion, finely chopped**
½ **green capsicum, white insides and**
   seeds removed, chopped
2 **stalks celery, sliced**
2 **bay leaves**
½ **teaspoon dried basil**
½ **teaspoon dried thyme**
½ **teaspoon dried oregano**
1 **x 400 g can Italian diced tomatoes**
1 **litre fish stock**
12 **okra, cut into 2 cm pieces**
12 **green (raw) king prawns, peeled and deveined,**
   tails intact
400 **g white fish fillets, such as blue-eye or john dory,**
   cut into 2–3 cm pieces
1–2 **raw blue swimmer crabs, cleaned and cut into**
   4–6 pieces or 100 g fresh crab meat (optional)
12 **oysters**
steamed rice, to serve
½ **cup chopped flat-leaf parsley, to serve**

Heat the oil in a small, preferably non-stick, saucepan and add the flour, stirring to make a roux. Cook, stirring with a wooden spoon, until the roux is a dark red/brown colour. Transfer to a large flameproof casserole dish and heat, then add the garlic, onion, capsicum and celery and cook for another couple of minutes.

Stir in the dried herbs and tomatoes, then add the stock a little at a time until the sauce thickens. Add the okra and cook for 10 minutes, then add the prawns, fish and crab pieces (if using) and cook very gently for 5 minutes. Add the oysters and crabmeat (if using) and cook for 1 minute more.

Serve with steamed rice and parsley sprinkled over.

INDIAN-SPICED JOHN DORY WITH CRISPY WONTON WRAPPERS AND MANGO RELISH
Serves 4

While this sounds exotic, it's not as much work as you might think. Leaving the mango seed in the relish during cooking releases the pectin, which helps thicken the relish.

2 **teaspoons ground coriander**
2 **teaspoons ground cumin**
1 **teaspoon ground turmeric**
1 **teaspoon salt**
4 **thin john dory fillets (120–150 g each)**
4–8 **wonton wrappers, depending on the size of the fish**
½–⅔ **cup neutral oil (see page 14)**
basmati rice, to serve

MANGO RELISH
1 **tablespoon neutral oil (see page 14)**
1 **red onion, roughly chopped**
1 **red capsicum, white insides and**
   seeds removed, roughly chopped
1 **red chilli, finely chopped**
1 **large mango, peeled, flesh cut into chunks,**
   seed reserved
1 **teaspoon grated ginger**
1 **teaspoon Indian curry powder**
1 **teaspoon ground coriander**
1 **tablespoon sugar**
2 **tablespoons white-wine vinegar**

Combine the spices and salt. Coat the fish fillets with the mixture, then cover and refrigerate for 2–4 hours.

For the relish, heat the oil in a saucepan and cook the onion, capsicum and chilli over medium heat until softened. Add the remaining ingredients, including the mango seed, and simmer for 15 minutes, adding a little water if necessary.

Place the wonton wrappers on the kitchen bench and brush with a little water. Gently press them onto the flesh side (not the skin side) of the fish.

Heat the oil in a large frying pan, add the fish (skin-side down) and cook, turning once, until the fish is cooked and the wonton pastry is golden and crisp – be careful, it will burn quickly, which is why you can't have very thick fillets. Drain well on paper towel, then serve with a generous amount of the relish and basmati rice.

ROAST SIRLOIN WITH BALSAMIC RED ONIONS AND MUSHROOM TARTS

Serves 4

This is dinner-party food for the family and it's easy to double the recipe if you're entertaining. If you are serving this as one of three courses, keep the other two light or have plenty of teenage boys involved, because this is a significant feed.

2 cloves garlic, crushed or grated
I tablespoon thyme leaves
⅓ cup olive oil
I tablespoon freshly ground black pepper
I × 800 g sirloin roast
4 red onions, peeled and quartered
½ cup balsamic vinegar

MUSHROOM TARTS
I teaspoon butter
I tablespoon olive oil
200 g portobello mushrooms, thickly sliced
I clove garlic, thinly sliced or crushed
I teaspoon thyme leaves
I tablespoon coarsely chopped pitted
    black olives
I tablespoon coarsely chopped
    sun-dried tomatoes
8 sheets frozen puff pastry, thawed and
    cut into 8 × 8–10 cm squares or rounds
I tablespoon pine nuts

Combine the garlic, thyme, 2 tablespoons olive oil and pepper in a bowl. Place the beef on a piece of plastic film and spoon the marinade over the top. Wrap up the beef and refrigerate for 12–24 hours, then bring to room temperature.

Preheat the oven to 220°C. Place the onion in a large roasting tin and toss with remaining olive oil and the balsamic vinegar. Put the beef on a rack in the tin and roast for about 45 minutes or until cooked to your liking. Remove from the oven and cover the whole dish with foil while the tarts are cooking.

To make the mushroom tarts, heat the butter and oil in a frying pan and cook the mushrooms and garlic over medium heat until browned but not cooked through. Transfer to a dish to prevent further cooking and add the thyme, olives and sun-dried tomatoes.

Line a tray with baking paper and place four pieces of pastry on the paper, without allowing them to touch. Top with a second piece of a pastry, crimp the edges together, then spoon the mushroom mixture (no juices) into the middle of each. Sprinkle with the pine nuts and bake for 10 minutes or until the pastry rises and turns golden brown.

Carve the beef and arrange on warm plates with the onion quarters and mushroom tarts. Pour any remaining mushroom juices into the pan the onions came from and then spoon over the meat.

‹ SUKIYAKI

Serves 4

You need to make a couple of investments to tackle this one. First, a small gas burner like they bring to the table in some Japanese restaurants (they're surprisingly cheap). Second, a cast-iron sukiyaki dish to sit on top (and these are surprisingly expensive). You will also need a trip to an Asian supermarket, ideally a Japanese one, to buy the frozen shaved beef, noodles and frozen grilled tofu. Please don't be intimidated by all this. It's a mile of fun for kids of all ages and you'll find that sukiyaki will become quite a regular treat.

Try this with steamed Japanese rice and a raw egg beaten in the bottom of your bowl (for the brave).

8 shiitake mushrooms
100 g enoki mushrooms (optional)
1 leek, white and pale-green parts only, thickly sliced
2 cups Chinese cabbage, cut into 3 cm pieces
1 cup shirataki or bean thread (cellophane) noodles
100 g yaki dofu (grilled tofu)
400–500 g shaved beef sirloin

STOCK
1 clove garlic, lightly crushed
1 thumb ginger, sliced
1 slice beef shin
½ cup soy sauce
½ cup sake
½ cup sugar

To make the stock, place the garlic, ginger, beef shin and 4 cups water in a saucepan. Bring to a boil, then reduce the heat and simmer gently for 2 hours, skimming any scum from the top. Strain through a fine sieve (you should have about 2 cups), then add the remaining ingredients and stir to dissolve the sugar.

Arrange all the other ingredients on one or two platters within reach of everyone. Ignite the gas burner and place the heavy sukiyaki dish on top. Pour a cup of the stock into the dish and add some of the mushrooms, leek and cabbage to further flavour the stock. When the leek has softened, add some noodles and tofu. Encourage everyone to put some vegetables in their bowl, then start adding the beef, cooking for only a few seconds to colour it. Keep adding ingredients until they're all used up.

CHORIZO AND OCTOPUS SALAD

Serves 4

At about 7 months of age, Zoe loved grilled baby octopus and used to gum them into submission. She went off them by the time she was 6, but I'm definitely sensing a comeback at the moment.

This is a terrific balance of textures and lovely strong flavours, probably best for teens (although it may appeal to the occasional toothless toddler).

8 small octopus (6–10 cm in diameter),
    head and 'beak' removed
2 cloves garlic, crushed
⅓ cup olive oil
8 small ripe roma tomatoes or 12 large
    cherry tomatoes, halved
1 teaspoon sugar
1 teaspoon dried thyme or 2 teaspoons
    fresh thyme leaves
1 butter lettuce, washed and dried
4 kipfler potatoes, steamed or boiled and peeled
2 chorizo sausages, sliced diagonally

DRESSING
½ cup extra virgin olive oil
¼ cup balsamic vinegar
12 mint leaves, finely sliced
½ bunch chives, finely sliced
sea salt and freshly ground black pepper

Place the octopus, garlic and 2 tablespoons olive oil in a bag or bowl and marinate in the fridge for 2–24 hours.

Preheat the oven to 120°C and line a baking tray with baking paper. Combine the tomato, sugar and thyme in a bowl, then place the tomatoes (cut-side up) on the baking tray and roast for 1 hour. Allow to cool completely.

Combine the dressing ingredients and set aside. Arrange the butter lettuce on a platter or four smaller plates and cut the potatoes into thick slices.

Chargrill the octopus over high heat. At the same time, heat the remaining olive oil in a frying pan over medium heat and cook the chorizo slices, turning once.

Arrange the chorizo, octopus, potato and tomato over the lettuce and spoon the dressing over the top.

CONFIT GARLIC PRAWNS
Serves 4

The trick here is to cook the garlic soooooo slowly to draw all its flavour into the olive oil before you add the prawns. It makes for a sauce that is so good you will mop up every drop of it with the bread.

1½ cups olive oil
16 cloves garlic
¼ teaspoon chilli flakes
I teaspoon sea salt
½ teaspoon freshly ground black pepper
12 large green (raw) king prawns,
    peeled and deveined, tails intact
2 teaspoons thyme leaves
I tablespoon pure thick cream
thick slices baguette, to serve

Place the oil and garlic in a small saucepan and bring to a very gentle simmer. Slowly cook the garlic until soft and golden, then add the chilli flakes and allow to cool.

Preheat the oven to 220°C. Purée the garlic mixture using a stab blender, then stir in the salt and pepper. Spoon the mixture into four small ovenproof dishes. Place the dishes on a baking tray and bake until sizzling (this will take about 10 minutes).

Add three prawns to each dish and stir to coat, then return to the oven for a few minutes until the prawns turn opaque.

Place the dishes on serving plates and top with thyme leaves and a teaspoon of cream. Serve with baguette.

ROAST HERB-ENCRUSTED CHICKEN ON PROVENÇALE VEGETABLES ›
Serves 4

Here's a double whammy of flavours from Provence, with both dried herbs and colourful Provençale vegetables.

½ cup olive oil
2 cloves garlic, finely sliced
I red capsicum, white insides and seeds removed,
    cut into 2 cm pieces
I green capsicum, white insides and seeds removed,
    cut into 2 cm pieces
I small yellow capsicum, white insides and seeds
    removed, cut into 2 cm slices
I large red onion, cut into 2 cm pieces
3 zucchini, cut into 2 cm slices
sea salt and freshly ground black pepper
4 chicken marylands, or I whole chicken, cut into
    8 pieces, trimmed of excess fat
40 g butter, melted
¼ cup dried Provençale herbs
I cup large red grapes
½ cup large pitted black olives
2 tablespoons red- or white-wine vinegar
I cup torn basil leaves
½ cup flat-leaf parsley leaves

Preheat the oven to 200°C. Place the olive oil, garlic, capsicum, onion and zucchini in a large baking dish and toss to coat well with the oil. Season with a little salt and pepper.

Pat the chicken pieces with paper towel and brush the skin side with melted butter. Sprinkle the dried herbs and I teaspoon sea salt over the chicken. Ideally, your baking dish will have a rack that will allow the chicken to sit over the veggies. If not, place the chicken pieces between the veg or just sit them on top. Roast for 40 minutes, then remove the chicken and keep warm.

Add the grapes, olives, vinegar, basil and parsley to the baking dish and cook for 5 minutes more.

Divide the chicken pieces and veggies among four warmed plates and serve.

STUFFED LAMB RACKS WITH SWEET POTATO PURÉE

Serves 4

Trick up an already delicious rack of lamb by splitting it lengthways and stuffing it with flavours that enhance the meat, not confuse it. The stuffing and tying process can be a family affair (often a shambles). Sweet potato purée makes the perfect accompaniment.

2 tablespoons sultanas
¼ cup marsala
70 g butter
I leek, white and pale-green parts only, finely sliced
I clove garlic, crushed or finely chopped
½ teaspoon cumin seeds
2 tablespoons thyme leaves
2 tablespoons toasted pine nuts
2 lamb racks (with 8 cutlets each), trimmed of fat
sea salt and freshly ground black pepper
400 g orange sweet potato, cut into even-sized pieces
I teaspoon ground cinnamon
steamed green vegetables, to serve

Combine the sultanas and marsala in a small bowl and soak for 20 minutes. Preheat the oven to 200°C.

Melt 20 g butter in a saucepan and cook the leek and garlic over medium heat until soft but not coloured. Add the cumin seeds and half the thyme leaves, then add the sultanas and marsala and simmer until the marsala evaporates. Stir in the pine nuts and allow to cool slightly.

Cut through the middle of each rack lengthways, almost to the bone.

Place a length of kitchen twine under every second rack (three lengths in all) and fill the cavities with the stuffing mixture. Tie with the twine and season well with salt and pepper. Bake for 15 minutes, then cover loosely with foil and leave to rest for about 10 minutes.

While the lamb is cooking, cook the sweet potato in boiling salted water until tender, then drain and mash. Add the cinnamon, remaining butter and remaining thyme leaves and mix well. Spoon onto four plates.

Remove the twine from the lamb and cut each rack in half. Divide the meat among the plates and serve with steamed greens (I love asparagus with this).

CROISSANT BREAD-AND-BUTTER PUDDING ›

Serves 4–6

English chef Antony Worrall Thompson attributes his rise to fame to the day 33 dozen croissants were delivered instead of the 3 dozen ordered. He was a 17-year-old pastry chef with a problem, but what a solution!

This is different from Thompson's recipe all those years ago, but the principle is the same. Just make sure that you buy crisp, buttery croissants from a proper patisserie, not the giant, flabby, doughy things from a service station.

2 tablespoons sultanas
2 tablespoons brandy, whisky or water
600 ml milk
400 ml pouring cream
I vanilla bean, split lengthways
3 organic or free-range eggs
6 organic or free-range egg yolks
200 g caster sugar
4 croissants, halved
½ cup demerara sugar
I teaspoon butter, softened
ice cream or whipped cream, to serve (optional)

Soak the sultanas in the brandy, whisky or water for 30 minutes.

Preheat the oven to 180°C and grease a ceramic baking dish that's large enough to hold the croissants (it's OK to pile them up a bit).

Combine the milk, cream and vanilla bean in a saucepan and bring to the verge of boiling. Remove from the heat and leave to infuse for a few minutes.

Beat the eggs, egg yolks and sugar in an electric mixer until pale. Remove the vanilla bean from the milk and cream, scraping all the seeds back into the liquid with a spoon. Pour into the egg mixture, whisking constantly so the eggs don't scramble. Add any liquid that the sultanas haven't absorbed.

Arrange the croissants in the baking dish, sprinkling the sultanas evenly throughout. Pour the custard mixture over the top, sprinkle with demerara sugar, dot with butter and bake for about 30 minutes or until the custard has just set – don't overcook it. Serve with ice cream or whipped cream, if desired.

GOOEY CHOCOLATE PUDDINGS
Serves 4

Even in a restaurant these have a great 'wow' factor. Make them a couple of times to get the knack and you won't believe how easy they are – or how seriously rich.

100 g butter, diced, plus extra for greasing
120 g dark chocolate (70% cocoa)
2 organic or free-range eggs
I organic or free-range egg yolk
120 g caster sugar
I teaspoon vanilla extract
30 g plain flour
ice cream or thickened cream, to serve

Preheat the oven to 190°C and grease four soufflé dishes with plenty of butter.

Melt the butter and chocolate very gently in a double boiler or in a bowl over a saucepan of barely simmering water (don't let the bottom of the bowl touch the water).

Beat the eggs, egg yolk, sugar and vanilla until they're pale yellow. Sift in the flour and beat until combined, then gently stir in the melted chocolate mixture.

Spoon into the soufflé dishes and place on a baking tray. Bake for 12–14 minutes or until the outside is cakey and the middle still molten (this is the bit that takes practice).

Serve with ice cream or thickened cream.

CHOCOLATE FONDUE ›
Serves 4

Kids really enjoy dipping and poking things at the table. Even better if there is chocolate involved. Here, you can take the vaguely healthy option by using fruit to dip, or go the whole hog and use marshmallows and maybe some firm cake as well.

fruit, such as strawberries, kiwi fruit and pineapple
marshmallows
cake or brioche

CHOCOLATE SAUCE
200 ml pouring cream
100 g dark chocolate (70% cocoa), broken into pieces
½ teaspoon vanilla extract

Bring the cream to a boil over medium heat in a small saucepan, then add the chocolate and vanilla and stir over very low heat until melted and smooth.

Serve with your choice of dippers.

Making Pasta

Good-quality dried pasta is cheap as chips and available just about everywhere. Really good-quality dried pasta is more expensive and harder to find, while good-quality fresh pasta is almost impossible to get. Making it at home isn't difficult, although you'd probably want to schedule in a couple of practice sessions before entertaining royalty. It isn't essential to have a pasta machine, but it sure helps.

Like bread and pizza, making pasta requires just a couple of basic ingredients and a little time and effort, but it's a heap of fun and can result in some seriously good eating. Have a go at making your own fresh pasta with your kids, then throw your family's favourite sauce on it. You'll be pretty chuffed with the results.

Pasta Fresco Bellissimo

Serves 4

200 g plain flour, plus extra for dusting
big pinch of pouring salt
2 organic or free-range eggs

Sift the flour and salt together onto a clean work surface. Make a well in the centre and break the eggs into it, then mix with your fingers to form a dough. Knead the dough for about 10 minutes – if it seems too thick, add a few drops of water; too soft, add a little more flour. Allow to rest for 20 minutes.

Roll out the dough very thinly on a well-dusted surface and cut into strips. Or, if you have a pasta machine, feed the dough through the rollers as instructed in the manual, then cut to size with the machine. Store over the back of a chair (not the velvet lounge chair) and use the same day.

Cook the pasta in lots of boiling salted water until al dente. It will cook much faster than dried pasta – usually just a couple of minutes.

IN MY DAY

In my day, we went around the world most Sunday nights. But we only ever went one place and that was China (unless Dad had had a shocker at the races – then it was a picnic on the lounge room floor, watching *Disneyland* and eating pikelets).

For not-very-adventurous eaters, Mum and Dad loved Chinese food. They had a lot of Chinese chums and this became their one area of culinary expertise. They knew to share dishes rather than order one each and they always accompanied the meal with lots of steamed rice. We would sit at laminex tables in Sydney's Chinatown, eating simple, honest food and thinking we were the luckiest people in the world.

Around The World

Keen to teach your kids about different cultures? Sick of cheese on toast every Sunday night? Well, here's an idea I pinched from some friends of ours. Every week the family goes out for a meal, sampling a new cuisine each time. Before they go, the kids research the country – the culture, the tucker and what life is like for kids their age. It's a great way to encourage them to try different ingredients, as well as do a little human geography.

If you live in Italy or France, where the cooking culture is strong and steeped in centuries of history, other cuisines are not always prominent. But in multicultural Australia, where the food was initially based on British and Irish food before the boom in immigration last century introduced us to many different European and Asian cultures, we have an amazing variety of cuisines to choose from.

Be as silly or as serious as you like. You can stick to the general takeaway cliches of, say, Chinese chicken-and-sweetcorn soup or beef chow mein, or you can delve deeper and explore a country's tucker, region by region.

Of course, you don't have to take the kids out to enjoy international cuisine. It's easy to recreate these dishes at home. Just pick a destination and send the kids off to do some research on the net (or, heaven forbid, in a book). Then cook up a storm and enjoy some new flavours together. It's about having fun and if they learn something along the way, that's no bad thing either.

Japan

Kids love sushi, and a lot of other Japanese dishes are pretty child-friendly too, like gyoza dumplings and fried tonkatsu pork. Take the kids on a quick trip to a Japanese food store to find exotic ingredients like miso paste, or to get a sushi mat – an essential tool for stress-free sushi-making. These days, many Japanese ingredients are also available at larger supermarkets.

Get the whole family involved with assembling the makimono or crumbing the pork for the tonkatsu and everyone will feel part of the process.

Gyoza: Tonkatsu pork
with Japanese potato salad

GYOZA
Makes 20

400 g finely minced premium lean pork
1 spring onion, pale and dark-green parts only,
    very finely chopped
⅓ cup cabbage, boiled until soft, then drained
    and finely chopped
1 teaspoon sugar
1 teaspoon grated ginger
1 organic or free-range egg, beaten
1 tablespoon Japanese soy sauce, plus extra
    for dipping
20 gyoza wrappers (available from Asian or
    Japanese food stores), or use round wheat (not egg)
    wonton wrappers, if unavailable
1 tablespoon neutral oil (see page 14)

Combine all the ingredients except the wrappers and oil
in a bowl and mix thoroughly with your hands.

Place a teaspoon of mixture inside each wrapper and
fold it in half. Secure the pastry by slightly wetting the
edge with a little water then pinching gently to seal.
As you finish each gyoza, place it on a board and push
down gently so the base flattens a bit.

Heat the oil in a heavy-based frying pan with a lid,
add the gyoza and fry until the bottom begins to brown.
Add ¼ cup water and cover with the lid. Reduce the heat
to low and cook for 5 minutes.

Remove the gyoza from the pan and allow to cool for a
minute before serving with Japanese soy sauce for dipping.

Pictured on previous page

TONKATSU PORK WITH JAPANESE POTATO SALAD
Serves 4

1 cup plain flour
1–2 organic or free-range eggs
2 cups Japanese breadcrumbs (panko)
4 Asian-cut pork cutlets (from an Asian butcher),
    bone removed or 1 thick pork fillet, cut into 1 cm slices
    and flattened slightly
1½ cups neutral oil (see page 14)
⅓–½ cup tonkatsu sauce
2 tablespoons white sesame seeds (optional)
finely shredded cabbage, to serve

POTATO SALAD
1 large desiree potato, peeled and cut into 1 cm dice
1 carrot, cut into 1 cm dice
1 small cucumber, peeled, seeds removed and
    cut into 1 cm dice (optional)
½ small red onion, very finely sliced
½ cup egg mayonnaise
1 tablespoon mirin
pinch of salt

To make the potato salad, boil the potato and carrot
in salted water until just tender. Add the cucumber
(if using) and onion and cook for 30 seconds more.
Drain and rinse under cold water, then leave to cool.
Mix through the mayo, mirin and salt.

Place the flour in a flat bowl. Beat the egg with a little
cold water in another bowl, and place the panko crumbs
in another. Coat the pork with the flour. Dip it in the egg,
then coat well with the breadcrumbs. Heat a little oil in
a frying pan and cook the pork over medium heat until
golden brown on both sides. Drain on paper towel.

Slice the pork and arrange on a plate, then pour
tonkatsu sauce over the top and sprinkle with sesame
seeds, if using. Serve on a bed of finely shredded cabbage
with the potato salad to the side.

Pictured on previous page

TERIYAKI CHICKEN

Serves 4

750 g chicken thigh fillets, skin-on, trimmed of excess fat
1 tablespoon neutral oil (see page 14)
steamed rice, to serve

MARINADE
1 teaspoon grated ginger
⅓ cup Japanese soy sauce
⅓ cup mirin
1 tablespoon sugar
2 tablespoons sake

Mix all the marinade ingredients together and add the chicken thighs, tossing to ensure they are completely covered. Cover and marinate in the fridge for one hour, then bring to room temperature.

Heat the oil in a frying pan with a lid, and add the chicken thighs (reserving the marinade), skin-side down, and cook over medium–high heat until the skin has browned. Turn the thighs over and add the reserved marinade, reduce the heat to low and cover, cooking until the chicken is cooked through (test this by piercing the thickest part of the thigh with a skewer – the juices should run clear).

Uncover and continue to cook for a minute or two over low heat until the sauce thickens slightly. Remove the chicken thighs and slice. Serve with plenty of sauce spooned over, accompanied by steamed rice.

SALMON OR TUNA ROLLS (MAKIMONO)

Makes 4 rolls

2 cups sushi rice
3–4 tablespoons seasoned rice vinegar
4 sheets nori
sushi mat, for rolling the nori (available from Japanese speciality stores)
½ cup shredded lettuce
½ small cucumber, thinly sliced
⅓ cup sashimi-grade raw salmon or tuna slices (about ½ cm thick)
¼ avocado, thinly sliced (optional)
2 tablespoons Japanese sushi mayo

Rinse the rice with water three times and drain well. Bring 3 cups water to a boil in a saucepan. Add the rice, turn the heat to low and simmer, covered, for 12–14 minutes until the rice is cooked, then drain well. (Alternatively, place in a rice cooker with 2 cups water and cook.) Once the rice is cooked, stir in the seasoned rice vinegar, cover with a clean tea towel and cool to room temperature.

Place a sheet of nori shiny-side down on a sushi mat, with the shorter side facing you. Leave about 1 cm between the end of the mat farthest from you and the nori. Wet your hands and take a handful of rice, placing it on the nori and spreading it out to the edges (but leaving a 1 cm gap at the edge farthest from you). The rice should lie on top of the nori in a thick slab, about two or three grains high.

Pile a quarter of the lettuce, cucumber, fish and avocado (if using) on the rice at the end nearest to you, leaving space around the edges so the filling is not pushed out when you roll it up. Dollop or squirt an even line of mayo on top. Pick up the mat at the near end and roll it up into a square shape, tapping the filling in at both ends with your fingers. Repeat with the remaining ingredients to make 4 rolls.

Wet the end of a very sharp knife, cut each roll into thick slices and serve immediately.

Thailand

Thai food for kids – are you mad, I hear you ask? There's no escaping the fact that Thai food generally features a lot of chilli, but there are exceptions, like pandan chicken, and you can, of course, leave the chilli out of other dishes if you are cooking for a younger family. However, Thai food is great for teenagers to enjoy as their tastes become a bit more adventurous. Try to get them to use their developing palates to balance the sweet, salty, sour and hot elements of Thai dishes – it's all part of the fun.

Pandan chicken

FISH CAKES

Makes 12–16

500 g snapper or other white fish fillets, skin and
    bones removed
1 tablespoon red curry paste
1 organic or free-range egg
2 tablespoons fish sauce
3 teaspoons grated palm sugar
3 green beans, very finely sliced
1 tablespoon finely chopped coriander
1 small red chilli, seeds removed and
    very finely sliced (optional)
½ cup neutral oil (see page 14)
sweet chilli sauce, to serve

Place the fish, curry paste, egg, fish sauce and palm sugar
in a food processor and process to a thick paste. Stir in
the beans, coriander and chilli (if using).

Form the mixture into walnut-sized balls and flatten
gently into a patty shape. Heat the oil in a frying pan and
cook the fish cakes until browned on both sides. Drain on
paper towel. Serve with sweet chilli sauce.

PANDAN CHICKEN

Serves 6 as an entrée

600 g chicken breasts or thigh fillets, trimmed
    and cut into 2 cm pieces
⅓ cup honey
2 teaspoons pouring salt
2 tablespoons fish sauce
1 teaspoon sesame oil
100 ml coconut milk (optional)
18 pandan leaves (available from specialist
    fruit shops and Asian food stores)
peanut oil or other neutral oil (see page 14),
    for pan-frying

PASTE
3 cloves garlic, sliced
2 sticks lemongrass, chopped
½ teaspoon ground turmeric
½ thumb ginger, peeled and sliced
2 coriander roots, washed

Pound the paste ingredients in a mortar and pestle or
blend in a food processor.

Place the paste, chicken, honey, salt, fish sauce, sesame
oil and coconut milk (if using) in a bowl and mix well.
Cover and marinate in the fridge for at least 2 hours.

Place two or three pieces of chicken on a pandan leaf
and wrap into neat triangular parcels, tying the leaf in a
knot around the chicken to secure, and trimming off any
excess. Repeat with remaining chicken and pandan leaves.
Fry in neutral oil until golden brown.

Pictured on previous page

CHICKEN AND COCONUT MILK SOUP
Serves 4

2 cups coconut milk
⅓ cup fish sauce
1 × 4 cm piece galangal, peeled and very finely sliced
12 kaffir lime leaves, halved
3 stalks lemongrass, very finely sliced
2 spring onions, white and pale-green parts only, thinly sliced on the diagonal
400 g chicken breasts, very thinly sliced
2 bird's eye chillies, seeds removed, finely sliced
⅓ cup fresh lime juice
½ cup coriander leaves

THAI CHICKEN STOCK
500 g chicken bones or wings
1 × 4 cm piece ginger, sliced
2 spring onions, white and pale-green parts only

To make the stock, throw all the ingredients into a stockpot with 2 litres water and bring to the boil. Reduce the heat and simmer for 1 hour, skimming any grey scum and excess oil from the top, then drain.

In a large heavy-based saucepan over medium–high heat, bring 2 cups of the stock or water, coconut milk and fish sauce to a simmer. Reduce the heat to low and add the galangal, kaffir lime leaves and lemongrass, cooking for about 15 minutes. Add the spring onion, chicken, chillies and lime juice and simmer for 2 minutes more, or until the chicken is cooked through.

Transfer to individual bowls to serve, garnished with coriander leaves.

PRAWN AND POMELO SALAD
Serves 4 as an entrée

¼ cup unsalted peanuts
neutral oil (see page 14), for cooking
12 green (raw) king prawns, peeled
150 g glass noodles
boiling water, to cover
1 small or ½ large pomelo (Thai grapefruit), peeled and segmented, segments chopped
½ cup coriander leaves
½ cup Vietnamese mint leaves

DRESSING
1 clove garlic, sliced
3 coriander roots, washed
2 red chillies, seeds removed
1 red bird's eye chilli, seeds removed
1 teaspoon sea salt
40 g palm sugar, finely chopped
2 tablespoons fish sauce
100 ml fresh lime juice

Lightly roast the peanuts in a dry frying pan over low heat until just browned, then transfer to a chopping board and roughly chop.

To make the dressing, blend the garlic, coriander roots, chillies and salt to a paste using a mortar and pestle or a food processor. Add the palm sugar, fish sauce and lime juice and stir well to thoroughly combine.

Heat a little neutral oil in a large frying pan and fry the prawns on both sides until opaque.

Meanwhile, place the noodles in a bowl and pour over enough boiling water to cover. Leave to stand for a minute or so until soft. Drain, then carefully cut in half with scissors or a sharp knife (to make them easier to eat).

In a large salad bowl, combine the prawns, noodles, pomelo, coriander and mint, and drizzle over the dressing. Top with the chopped peanuts and serve.

France

France may be one unified country, but food-wise it is dozens of mini nations each with their own regional produce and culinary specialties. Kids can learn a lot about these regional differences and their origins through food. Start in Normandy, famous for its apples and cream, through Paris with its classic bistro fare, down to the Mediterranean with its tomatoes, capsicums, olives and oil, then head west for the fabulous bouillabaisse from St Tropez or Marseilles.

French onion soup, Paris-bistro style

COQ AU VIN
Serves 4

⅓ cup plain flour
1 teaspoon pouring salt
½ teaspoon freshly ground black pepper
1 free-range or organic chicken, backbone removed,
    cut into 8 pieces, or 4 chicken marylands
150 g thick rashers streaky bacon, rind removed
2 fresh bay leaves
4 stalks flat-leaf parsley
8 sprigs thyme
2 tablespoons olive oil
75 g butter
8–12 pickling onions (also known as pearl onions)
3 cups red wine
1 cup chicken stock
1 small whole head garlic, halved crossways
150 g button mushrooms, left whole if small or
    halved if medium-sized
2 tablespoons coarsely chopped flat-leaf parsley
boiled or mashed potatoes, to serve

Preheat the oven to 170°C. Combine the flour, salt and pepper in a large plastic bag, then add the chicken pieces and shake well to coat. Place the bacon in a saucepan and cover with cold water. Bring to a boil, then reduce the heat and simmer for 2 minutes. Drain and cut into 5 mm wide lardons.

Wrap bay leaves, parsley stalks and thyme in muslin and secure with kitchen twine to make a bouquet garni.

Heat the olive oil and two-thirds of the butter in a heavy-based casserole dish with a lid. Add the chicken pieces and brown well on both sides, then remove to a plate. Add the onions and cook until browned, then transfer to the plate with the chicken pieces. Add the bacon and brown. Sprinkle on any flour remaining in the bag and stir to mix with the bacon and fat in the pan. Return the chicken and onions to the casserole and add the wine, chicken stock, garlic and bouquet garni. Bring to a boil, cover with the lid and cook for 1 hour.

Remove the garlic and bouquet garni and set aside for 10 minutes. While the casserole is resting, quickly fry the mushrooms in the remaining butter and add to the dish.

Serve the coq au vin sprinkled with chopped parsley and accompanied by boiled or mashed potatoes.

FRENCH ONION SOUP, PARIS-BISTRO STYLE
Serves 4

50 g butter
1.5 kg brown onions, halved and
    sliced lengthways (not across)
2 cloves garlic, finely sliced
1 tablespoon plain flour
4 cups beef stock
1 tablespoon brandy (optional)
1 fresh bay leaf
4 sprigs thyme and 2 stalks parsley, tied with
    kitchen twine
sea salt and freshly ground black pepper
4–8 slices baguette, depending on
    the size of your soup bowls
150 g gruyère cheese, grated

Melt the butter in a large heavy-based saucepan, then add the onion and garlic and gently cook over low heat for about 30 minutes until very soft and golden. Stir in the flour and cook for another couple of minutes, then add the beef stock, 1 cup water, brandy, bay leaf, thyme and parsley stalks and 1 teaspoon salt. Bring to a boil, then reduce to a simmer and cook for 1 hour. Taste and season with pepper and a little more salt if necessary.

Place four individual tureens, large soufflé dishes or ovenproof soup bowls on a baking tray. Lightly toast the baguette slices.

Ladle the soup evenly into the four bowls, discarding the bay leaf and herbs. Place the toasted baguette slices on top of the soup and generously sprinkle with grated gruyère. Arrange your oven racks so the top of the soup is 4–6 cm from the grill, then grill until the cheese melts and starts to brown.

Allow to cool for a few minutes before serving.

Pictured on previous page

MOULES MARINIERES
Serves 4

I teaspoon butter
2 red shallots, finely chopped
I clove garlic, finely chopped
2 bay leaves
4 sprigs thyme, leaves picked
4 stalks flat-leaf parsley, stalks and
    leaves separated, leaves finely sliced
150 ml white wine
¼–⅓ cup cream
I kg small black mussels, beards removed,
    any open shells discarded
freshly ground black pepper
crusty bread, to serve

In a large stockpot with a lid, melt the butter, then add the shallots and garlic, frying for a minute or so to soften. Add the bay leaves, thyme leaves, parsley stalks, white wine and cream and bring to a boil. Throw in the mussels, cover and cook for a few minutes, shaking the pot occasionally.

When most of the mussels have opened, add the parsley leaves and season well with black pepper. Cover again and cook for another minute or so until all the mussels have opened.

Remove the parsley stalks and bay leaves before serving the mussels with plenty of sauce, accompanied by crusty bread.

LEEKS GRATIN
Serves 4

8–12 baby leeks (if you can find them) or 4 large leeks,
    white and pale-green parts only, well washed and
    halved lengthways
I cup grated emmental or gruyère cheese
¼ teaspoon nutmeg
sea salt and freshly ground black pepper
¾ cup cream
crusty bread and a green salad, to serve

Preheat the oven to 200°C and lightly grease a baking dish.

Bring a large pan of water to a boil. Briefly plunge the leeks in for 30 seconds or so to blanch, then drain on paper towel. Place them in the prepared dish and scatter the cheese then the nutmeg over. Season well and pour the cream over evenly.

Bake for 10–15 minutes until the cheese is golden-brown and the leeks are cooked through.

Serve with crusty bread and a green salad.

India

Enjoying the immensely varied cuisine of India is a bit like a history lesson. Discover a little about the country's past and how the hundreds of semi-independent regions and British-ruled areas eventually morphed into the vast melting pot we call India. Still today, the colder Kashmir region has a very different approach to food from the coastal region of Goa where the cuisine is based on seafood. Here are a few basic recipes to get you started – get into the swing of things with these and then you can broaden your horizons.

Tandoori prawns

TANDOORI PRAWNS

Serves 4 as an entrée

6 cardamom pods
1 tablespoon sweet paprika
½ teaspoon ground cumin
2 teaspoons ground turmeric
½ teaspoon salt
1 tablespoon grated ginger
2 cloves garlic, grated or crushed
2 tablespoons lemon juice
¼ cup natural yoghurt
12 large green (raw) prawns,
    peeled and deveined, tails intact
lemon wedges, to serve

Crush the cardamom pods in a mortar and pestle and add the paprika, cumin, turmeric, salt, ginger, garlic and lemon juice. Mix well, then stir in the yoghurt.

Coat the prawns with the mixture and refrigerate for 1–4 hours.

Bring the prawns to room temperature and barbecue or pan-fry until they are opaque – be careful not to overcook. Serve with lemon wedges.

Pictured on previous page

INDIAN RICE PUDDING

Serves 6–8

½ cup long-grain rice
1.25 litres milk, plus extra if needed
150 g sugar
½ teaspoon saffron threads
seeds from 9 cardamom pods, crushed in
    a mortar and pestle
20 g butter
½ cup slivered almonds
½ cup raisins
thickened cream, to serve (optional)

Combine the rice, milk, sugar, saffron and ground cardamom seeds in a large saucepan. Bring to a boil, then reduce the heat and simmer for 40 minutes, adding a little more milk if needed. Keep a close eye on it during cooking so the rice doesn't burn on the base of the pan.

Melt the butter in a small saucepan and brown the almonds. Add the raisins and stir to coat, then add to the rice and mix well.

Serve in individual bowls with or without a dollop of thickened cream.

BUTTER CHICKEN

Serves 4

¾ cup whole cashew nuts
800 g chicken thigh fillets or breasts,
    cut into 3–4 cm pieces
⅓ cup neutral oil (see page 14)
1 small brown onion, very finely chopped
1 stick cinnamon
1 teaspoon sea salt
1 teaspoon sweet paprika
2 tablespoons tomato paste
250 ml pouring cream
1 bay leaf
½ teaspoon chilli powder (optional)
steamed rice, to serve

MARINADE
100 ml natural yoghurt
2 cloves garlic, crushed
1 teaspoon grated ginger
1 teaspoon garam masala
1 teaspoon ground cumin
1 teaspoon ground turmeric
½ teaspoon ground cardamom

Lightly roast the nuts in a dry frying pan over low heat until just browned. Transfer a third of the nuts to a mortar and grind them to a powder, reserving the whole nuts.

Combine all the marinade ingredients in a shallow dish and add the chicken. Cover and marinate in the fridge for at least 4 hours or overnight if you have time.

Bring the marinated chicken to room temperature. Heat half the oil over medium–high heat in a deep frying pan or a wok and brown the chicken (reserving the marinade), then drain on paper towel and set aside.

Wipe the pan or wok clean and add the remaining oil. Add the onion and soften over medium–high heat, then add the rest of the ingredients including the chilli powder, if using.

Simmer for a few minutes before adding the chicken, reserved marinade and ground cashews, stirring to combine. Simmer for 10–15 minutes until the chicken is just cooked through. Stir through the whole roasted cashews and serve with steamed rice.

GOAN-STYLE FISH CURRY

Serves 4

2 tablespoons neutral oil (see page 14)
8 cloves
6 cardamom pods, lightly crushed
1 brown onion, sliced
1½ tablespoons tamarind paste
6 fresh curry leaves (optional)
300 ml coconut cream
400 ml coconut milk
750 g firm white fish such as whiting, ling or perch,
    cut into 4 cm pieces
sea salt and freshly ground black pepper
steamed rice, to serve

CURRY PASTE
100 g shredded coconut
6 cloves garlic
1 × 4 cm piece ginger, peeled and sliced
6 dried red chillies
1 teaspoon cumin seeds
½ teaspoon ground turmeric

Using a large mortar and pestle or a food processor, blend all the curry paste ingredients to a smooth paste.

Heat the oil in a large frying pan over medium heat, then add the paste. Fry for 5 minutes, stirring constantly, until aromatic. Add the cloves, cardamom, onion, tamarind paste, curry leaves, coconut cream and milk and ½ cup water and simmer for a few minutes.

Add the fish, season well and simmer for a few minutes until the fish is cooked through. Serve with steamed rice.

Malaysia

Our Asian neighbour's food is becoming more and more popular in Australia. However, like Thai food, it is a cuisine that can be pretty intimidating heat-wise for younger kids. For those old enough though, Malaysian cuisine is a joy – the robust flavours of the laksas, curries and noodle dishes are amazing. As well as cooking these dishes at home, a search to find the best laksa in town (whether in a food hall, a restaurant or the humblest cafe) is a very worthwhile culinary crusade in its own right. As far as my family go, we rate Sentosa's, in Sydney's Crows Nest, as our favourite in town, and their chicken curry (see page 159) is even better.

Beef rendang

KAPITAN CHICKEN
Serves 4

600 g chicken thigh fillets, trimmed and
    cut into 2–3 cm pieces
2 tablespoons plain flour
½ cup neutral oil (see page 14)
400 ml coconut milk
2 pieces cassia bark or 1 stick cinnamon
2 tablespoons desiccated coconut,
    lightly toasted in a dry frying pan
steamed rice, to serve

PASTE
1 tablespoon coriander seeds
1 teaspoon cumin seeds
1 star anise
½ teaspoon freshly grated nutmeg
1 teaspoon sea salt
3 cloves garlic, roughly chopped
½ thumb ginger, peeled and chopped
1 small piece fresh turmeric, chopped or
    ½ teaspoon ground turmeric
4 spring onions, white and pale-green
    parts only, chopped
1 teaspoon belachan (dried shrimp paste),
    fried in a pan for a minute
6–8 dried small red chillies, seeds removed if you like

To make the paste, grind the dry spices in a mortar and pestle, then combine with the remaining ingredients (or throw the lot in a food processor).

Dust the chicken pieces with the flour. Heat the oil in a wok until very hot and cook the chicken until just brown but not cooked through. Drain on paper towel.

Fry the paste in a little of the oil and add the coconut milk and cassia bark or cinnamon stick. Bring to a boil, then reduce the heat and simmer for about 5 minutes until the chicken is nearly cooked through. Stir through the toasted coconut and simmer for another couple of minutes. Serve with steamed rice.

BEEF RENDANG
Serves 4

2 dried small red chillies
1 thumb ginger, peeled and chopped
1 stick lemongrass, thick white part only, chopped
1 clove garlic, chopped
1 large brown onion, sliced
2 tablespoons neutral oil (see page 14)
600 g topside or blade steak, trimmed of fat
    and cut into 3 cm cubes
¼ cup desiccated coconut, lightly toasted
    in a dry frying pan
1 teaspoon pouring salt
2 teaspoons sweet paprika
1 teaspoon Malay curry powder
2 × 270 ml cans coconut milk
½ cup water, plus extra if needed
steamed rice, to serve

Soak the dried chillies in hot water for 10 minutes, then drain and chop. Place in a food processor with the ginger, lemongrass, garlic and onion and blend to a thick paste.

Heat the oil in a wok or saucepan and fry the paste for a couple of minutes, until fragrant. Add the beef and desiccated coconut and stir to combine, then add the salt, paprika and curry powder. Cook for 1 minute, then stir in the coconut milk and water. Bring to a boil, then reduce the heat and simmer very gently for 2 hours uncovered, stirring occasionally. Add a little more water if the mixture starts to dry out. Serve with steamed rice.

Pictured on previous page

SENTOSA'S CHICKEN CURRY
Serves 4–6

1 tablespoon neutral oil (see page 14)
1½ tablespoons **Malay curry powder**
1 teaspoon ground cumin
1 teaspoon ground coriander
½ teaspoon ground turmeric
½ cup tomato sauce
400 ml coconut milk
1 teaspoon sea salt, or more to taste
1 teaspoon sugar, or more to taste
1 whole chicken, boned and cut into 12 pieces
   or 1 kg chicken breasts (halved) or thighs
steamed rice, to serve

CURRY PASTE
1 red onion, finely chopped
1 stalk lemongrass, finely sliced
1 × 2 cm piece ginger, peeled and sliced
50 g candlenuts

Blend the curry paste ingredients to a smooth paste using a mortar and pestle or food processor.

Heat the oil in a large heavy-based pan over medium heat. Add the curry paste, curry powder and ground spices and cook for a few minutes until aromatic. Stir through the tomato sauce, coconut milk, ¾ cup water and salt and sugar to taste, then add the chicken pieces and simmer for about 30 minutes, until the chicken is cooked through. Serve with steamed rice.

SNAKEBEANS WITH TOMATO AND CHILLI
Serves 4–6 as a side dish

2 tablespoons neutral oil (see page 14)
1 bunch snakebeans, cut into 3–4 cm lengths
2 cloves garlic, sliced
6 ripe cherry tomatoes, halved
2 spring onions, white and pale-green parts only, sliced
1 red chilli, sliced
2 tablespoons kecap manis

Heat the oil in a wok over high heat and add all the ingredients except for the kecap manis. Stir-fry for a minute or so, then stir through the kecap manis and simmer for 1 minute before serving.

Morocco

Working on the fringes of the food business, I've learned what an enormous effect one chef can have on the popularity of a cuisine – think Neil Perry with modern Asian or David Thompson with Thai. Likewise, Greg Malouf has almost singlehandedly championed quality Middle Eastern food and taught a lot of other chefs to spread the message. His books are a pretty good place to start exploring beyond the clichés of Moroccan food, with its wonderful complexities and subtleties. Or try my recipes on the following pages.

Chicken tagine with preserved lemon

CHICKEN TAGINE WITH PRESERVED LEMON

Serves 4

1 cup plain flour
sea salt and freshly ground black pepper
1 large free-range or organic chicken, backbone
   removed, cut into 8 pieces
½ cup olive oil, plus 2 tablespoons extra
4 cloves garlic, sliced
2 large brown onions, sliced
½ teaspoon saffron threads
1 stick cinnamon
1 teaspoon ground ginger
1 teaspoon ground cumin
1 tablespoon honey
½ cup blanched almonds
4 large kipfler potatoes, peeled and halved
2 preserved lemons, pulp discarded, rind chopped
2 tablespoons currants
2 cups homemade chicken stock (or 1 cup stock
   from a tetra pack, mixed with 1 cup water)
12 green beans, cut into 3 cm lengths
12 black or green pitted olives
1 cup coriander leaves
2 tablespoons chopped flat-leaf parsley
steamed couscous, to serve

Season the flour with salt and pepper, then use to dust the chicken pieces. Heat the olive oil in a large frying pan and cook the chicken over medium heat until golden brown. Drain on paper towel.

Heat the extra oil in a large heavy-based saucepan with a lid and soften the garlic and onion without browning. Add the saffron, cinnamon, ginger, cumin, honey, almonds, potato, preserved lemon, currants, stock and the chicken pieces. Bring to a boil, then reduce to the gentlest simmer. Cover the surface with baking paper, place the lid on the pan and simmer for 30 minutes.

Remove the lid and the paper. Add the beans and olives and simmer for 5 minutes more. Add the fresh herbs and serve with couscous.

Pictured on previous page

HARIRA

Serves 4

2 tablespoons olive oil
400 g lamb shoulder or leg, cut into 1 cm dice
2 cloves garlic, chopped
1 large brown onion, chopped
1 small red onion, sliced
1 teaspoon ground turmeric
1 teaspoon ground cumin
½ teaspoon ground ginger
1 stick cinnamon
150 g green lentils
1 × 400 g can Italian diced tomatoes
sea salt and freshly ground black pepper
100 g angel hair pasta or egg fettucine,
   broken into small pieces
1 × 400 g can chickpeas, drained
2 tablespoons chopped coriander

Heat the oil in a large saucepan over high heat and brown the lamb pieces. Add the garlic and brown and red onion and cook until soft but not coloured. Stir in the turmeric, cumin, ginger, cinnamon and lentils, then add the tomato and 1.25 litres water. Season with salt and pepper. Bring to a boil, then reduce the heat and simmer for 1½ hours, covered with a sheet of baking paper.

Remove the baking paper and add the pasta and chickpeas. Cook for another 10–15 minutes until the pasta is al dente.

Remove from the heat and add the coriander. Check the seasoning and serve in soup bowls.

MIDDLE EASTERN MUSSEL AND CHICKPEA STEW

Serves 4–6

¼ cup olive oil
1 leek, white part only, well washed,
    quartered lengthways and sliced
3 cloves garlic, finely sliced
2 teaspoons ground cumin
1 teaspoon ground coriander
1 teaspoon sweet paprika
1 stick cinnamon
½ teaspoon freshly ground black pepper
¼ teaspoon cayenne pepper
1 × 400 g can chickpeas, drained
1 × 400 g Italian diced tomatoes or
    2 cups chopped ripe tomatoes
2 kg small black mussels, beards removed,
    any open shells discarded
½ cup coriander leaves
2 tablespoons lemon juice
crusty bread, to serve

Heat the oil in a large stockpot over medium heat, then add the leek, garlic and all the spices, frying until the leek is softened. Add the chickpeas and tomato and simmer for 10 minutes.

Throw in the mussels, cover and increase the heat to high, cooking for a few minutes and shaking the pot every now and then. Check to see that all the mussels have opened – if not, return the lid to the pot and cook for a few minutes more.

When the mussels are cooked, stir through the coriander and the lemon juice and serve immediately with some crusty bread.

LAMB SHANKS WITH SWEET POTATO AND FIGS

Serves 4

1 cup plain flour
1 teaspoon pouring salt
4 lamb shanks, trimmed of excess fat
⅓ cup olive oil, plus extra if needed
3 cloves garlic, chopped
2 brown onions, sliced
2 sticks cinnamon
2 teaspoons ground coriander
1 tablespoon ground cumin
½ teaspoon ground turmeric
200 g green or blue dried lentils
2 cups chicken stock
500 g sweet potato, peeled and cut into 3 cm cubes
½ cup raisins
100 g dried figs
1 cup coriander leaves, roughly chopped
steamed couscous, to serve

Place the flour and salt in a plastic bag and, one by one, add the lamb shanks and shake until completely coated in flour, shaking off any excess.

In a large heavy-based flameproof casserole, heat the oil over medium–high heat and brown the shanks on all sides. Remove and set aside to drain on paper towel.

Add the garlic and onion to the pan (adding a little more oil if necessary) and fry over medium heat until softened. Add the spices and stir well to incorporate. Return the shanks to the casserole and add the lentils, chicken stock and enough water to just cover the ingredients. Cover with a sheet of baking paper and place the lid on the casserole.

Bring to a boil then simmer for 1¼ hours. Add the sweet potato, raisins and figs, then cover and simmer for another 30 minutes or until the potato is soft but not mushy. Garnish with coriander and serve with couscous.

Spain

It was only a few years ago that you really had to look hard to find **authentic** Spanish restaurants in Australia. Now, with the arrival of Bodega in Sydney and Movida in Melbourne, among others, Spanish is the new black (well, the new Italian anyway) – and quite possibly the hottest cuisine in the world. Jamón is certainly the new prosciutto, with jamón ibérico from free-range, acorn-fed pigs being ever so trendy. Making your own empanadas (the Spanish version of the pastie) is a breeze and kids will love them. Paella, the Spanish staple, is a treasure trove of delicious ingredients.

Seafood paella

SEAFOOD PAELLA
Serves 4

1 litre homemade or premium packaged fish stock
   (or 2 cups from a tetra pack, mixed with 2 cups water)
1 teaspoon saffron threads
1/3 cup olive oil
200 g firm white fish fillets, cut into 2–3 cm pieces
4 small baby octopus, cleaned and quartered
1 large onion, finely sliced
2 cloves garlic, finely sliced
2 cups Spanish calasparra rice
2 teaspoons Spanish smoked paprika
1 teaspoon sea salt
12 green (raw) prawns, peeled and deveined, tails intact
12 mussels, beards removed
1 tube good-quality squid, sliced
1/2 cup frozen peas
12 ripe cherry tomatoes, halved
1 tablespoon chopped coriander
1 tablespoon chopped flat-leaf parsley
freshly ground black pepper

Heat the stock over medium heat and add the saffron, simmering for a minute or two to break down the saffron.

Heat a paella pan to hot, then add half the oil and quickly brown the fish and octopus without cooking them. Remove from the pan.

Heat the remaining oil in the pan and add the onion, garlic and rice, stirring to soften the onion. Add the paprika and salt and cook for another minute, then stir in the stock and cook for about 5 minutes. Add the seafood, peas and tomato and stir gently without disturbing the bottom of the paella pan (you want this to be crisp).

When the rice is al dente and the seafood is just cooked, sprinkle over the coriander and parsley and finish with a good grinding of pepper. Serve immediately.

Pictured on previous page

EMPANADAS
Makes 24

1 tablespoon olive oil
1 clove garlic, crushed
1/2 onion, finely chopped
500 g premium minced beef
1/2 teaspoon ground oregano
1 teaspoon pouring salt
1/2 teaspoon ground coriander
1/2 teaspoon ground cumin
1 × 400 g can Italian diced tomatoes
2 tablespoons raisins
6 stuffed olives, chopped
2 hard-boiled eggs, coarsely chopped
6 sheets frozen shortcrust pastry, thawed

Preheat the oven to 200°C and line a baking tray with baking paper.

Heat the olive oil in a frying pan and cook the garlic and onion until soft but not coloured. Add the beef and brown for a few minutes, breaking up any lumps. Stir in the oregano, salt, coriander and cumin, then add the tomato and raisins. Simmer for 10 minutes until the liquid has reduced slightly. Remove the pan from the heat and set aside to cool, then stir through the chopped olives and hard-boiled egg.

Using a small bowl approximately 10 cm in diameter, cut out four rounds from each pastry sheet with a sharp knife. Spoon a tablespoon of the cooled filling into the middle of each round. Brush a little milk or water around the edges of the pastry rounds, then bring the edges together and pinch to seal.

Arrange the empanadas on the prepared tray and cook on the top shelf of the oven for 15 minutes or until golden brown and crisp all over. Transfer to a wire rack to cool just a little before eating.

SPANISH BEEF CASSEROLE
Serves 4

1.2 kg chuck or topside, cut into 3–4 cm chunks
1 small onion, peeled
2 bay leaves
2 tablespoons ground cumin
1 heaped teaspoon pouring salt
1 heaped teaspoon freshly ground black pepper
¼ cup cider vinegar
2 tablespoons olive oil
1 large brown onion, sliced
3 cloves garlic, sliced
1 heaped teaspoon smoked paprika
½ cup tomato purée or passata
2 large carrots, sliced into 2 cm chunks
2 waxy potatoes, cut into 2–3 cm chunks

Place the beef, whole onion, bay leaves, cumin, salt, pepper and vinegar in a large heavy-based flameproof casserole and cover with water. Place a sheet of baking paper on top, cover with the lid, then bring to a boil over high heat before reducing the heat to very low and simmering for 1½ hours. Carefully drain the contents of the casserole through a colander, discarding the liquid, whole onion and bay leaf, and setting aside the beef.

Heat the oil in the casserole over medium heat. Add the sliced onion and garlic and fry over medium heat for a few minutes until golden. Add the beef to the pan along with the smoked paprika, tomato purée or passata, carrots and potatoes, and fill with water to just cover, stirring to combine. Place a fresh sheet of baking paper over the casserole, cover with the lid, turn the heat to low and simmer for 30–40 minutes. Serve.

PAN-FRIED SNAPPER WITH ROMESCO SAUCE
Serves 4

½ cup olive oil
2 cloves garlic, finely sliced
1 tablespoon sherry vinegar
4 spinach leaves, stalks discarded, roughly chopped
4 × 180–200 g snapper or other white fish fillets, skin on

ROMESCO SAUCE
½ cup blanched almonds
½ cup coarse white breadcrumbs
¼ cup olive oil
1 small red onion, sliced
1 red capsicum
2 ripe tomatoes
2 cloves garlic
pinch of cayenne pepper (optional)
1 tablespoon sherry vinegar
½ teaspoon sugar
½ teaspoon sea salt
½ teaspoon freshly ground black pepper

To make the romesco sauce, lightly roast the almonds and breadcrumbs in a dry frying pan, then reserve. In the same pan, add 1 tablespoon of the oil and fry the onion until softened, then reserve. Chargrill the capsicum until blackened, then place in a paper bag and seal for a minute or two. When cool enough to handle, remove the charred skin, white insides and seeds and cut the flesh into strips.

Bring a small pan of water to a boil, and fill a small bowl with iced water. Cut an 'X' into the base of each tomato, then drop into boiling water for 15 seconds, before transferring to iced water for a further 15 seconds. Peel off the skin and roughly chop. Place all the sauce ingredients (including remaining olive oil) into a food processor and blend to a thick sauce, adding water, a tablespoon at a time, if needed.

In a large heavy-based pan, heat half the oil over medium heat and soften the garlic. Add the sherry vinegar and spinach along with 2 tablespoons water and cook for a minute or two until the spinach is soft. Meanwhile, in another pan, heat the remaining oil and cook the fish over medium heat, skin-side down first, for a few minutes until cooked through.

Serve the fish fillets with a spoonful of romesco sauce and a little of the spinach alongside.

IN MY DAY

In my day – and, happily, still to this day – Christmas is about the family coming together and giving presents to the kids (we gave up on the grown-ups' socks-and-underwear exchange years ago), before everyone pitches in with their contribution to lunch: Aunty Joy's rice salad, Sue's sausage rolls, Dad's bland roast chooks (and the ham that he and Mum win at bingo), while my brother and I do something smarty-pants and different each year.

As far as birthdays go, one of my favourite childhood memories is of my 5th birthday party. My friend George discovered a dozen iced donuts hanging from the Hills hoist in preparation for a party game, while the rest of us were still indoors, eagerly pinning the tail on the donkey. We went outside to find George chewing away on the last donut, looking surprised but not particularly guilty. Forty-seven years later, George and I are still great mates – but I'm not silly enough to share my donuts with him.

Family Celebrations

I reckon that even if you think you love big family gatherings, you probably hate them a bit at the same time. (And I also reckon that if you say you really hate them, you love them a bit too.) They're like that: wonderful on the one hand and horrible on the other.

Every family gathering has screaming kids playing and adults telling them to be quiet; Mum doing all the work for the barbecue and Dad taking all the glory; an uncle who has drunk too much and a teenager trying to sneak a beer; grandparents snoozing with limp paper plates still in their laps . . .

There is always too much food. Everyone pitches in: one aunt brings her famous rice salad, another her celebrated pavlova; and the third aunt brings her curried something-or-other that everyone loathes but has been too polite to say so for the past 20 years.

I try to make the big get-togethers, like Christmas, a bit easier by having just a couple of simple, quality dishes, but at the end of the day families want tradition. It doesn't necessarily have to be roast turkey, just whatever the traditional meal is for your family.

No-fuss Christmas

There are lots of terrific books with recipes for giant stuffed turkeys with all the trimmings, glazed hams and traditional Christmas puds. This isn't one of them.

It's likely to be a thousand degrees, you've been up half the night assembling a bike, trampoline or cubby house and you have to cope with several relatives with whom this once-a-year contact is once too much. Do you really need the extra grief of a turkey one size larger than your oven?

Let's keep things easy. No panic, no fuss and no lather of sweat. Cold starter (gazpacho courtesy of Stephanie Alexander's wonderful *The Cook's Companion*, made even more special by the addition of seafood and guacamole), a couple of yummy barbecue dishes and a cold dessert. Plenty of time for afternoon naps and playing with your kids. It really is Christmas.

Barbecued oregano prawns; Back-to-front
marinated beef with chargrilled asparagus

GAZPACHO WITH AVOCADO AND SHELLFISH

1.5 kg really ripe tomatoes, coarsely chopped
200 g cucumber, peeled, seeded and chopped
150 g red capsicum, white insides and seeds removed,
**   coarsely chopped**
2 cloves garlic, sliced
100 g crustless sourdough bread
2 cups cold water
3 teaspoons sea salt
freshly ground black pepper or Tabasco sauce, to taste
½ cup sherry vinegar
½ cup extra virgin olive oil
cooked crab meat, prawns, yabbies or lobster, to serve

GUACAMOLE OF SORTS
2 ripe, firm avocados, seed removed, flesh finely diced
1 small red onion, very finely chopped
1 tomato, peeled, seeded and finely chopped
freshly ground black pepper
a few drops of Tabasco

Process the vegetables, garlic and bread in a food
processor and transfer to a bowl. Stir in the water,
salt, pepper and vinegar, then cover and refrigerate for
at least an hour. Add the olive oil and check the seasoning
before serving.

Combine the guacamole ingredients and lightly mash
with a fork. Place a little in the centre of shallow bowls
and top with the seafood. Carefully pour the gazpacho
around the guacamole and serve immediately.

Note: The last step may be done at the table if you have
a jug or tureen flash enough for the task.

BARBECUED OREGANO PRAWNS

24 large green (raw) king prawns,
**   peeled and deveined, tails intact**
1 tablespoon dried oregano leaves or
**   whole dried oregano, crumbled**
¼ cup extra virgin olive oil
very finely grated zest of ½ a lemon
½ teaspoon sea salt
½ teaspoon freshly ground black pepper
lemon wedges, to serve

Combine all the ingredients and mix until the prawns are
well coated. Cover and place in the fridge for 1 hour.

Chargrill or barbecue the prawns for a minute or two
on each side until just cooked. Serve with lemon wedges.

Pictured on previous page

BACK-TO-FRONT MARINATED BEEF WITH CHARGRILLED ASPARAGUS

1–1.2 kg rump steak in a single piece or
   2–3 very thick sirloin steaks
1 cup extra virgin olive oil
sea salt and freshly ground black pepper
3 bunches asparagus, woody ends discarded
3 cloves garlic, crushed
3 anchovy fillets, finely chopped
2 tablespoons finely chopped rosemary
finely grated zest and juice of ½ a lemon

Brush the steak on both sides with a little of the oil and season well with salt and pepper.

Chargrill the steak over medium heat (it's a thick lump of meat and you don't want it black as charcoal) for 10–15 minutes each side until it is rare or medium–rare. When you turn the meat, place the asparagus spears on the chargrill and cook until they begin to soften.

When the meat is nearly done, pour 1 tablespoon olive oil into a small baking tray and place it on the barbecue. Add the garlic and anchovies and stir until the anchovies 'melt' and the garlic is pale golden brown. Add the rosemary and the rest of the oil and heat until just warmed through. Stir in the lemon zest and juice and plenty of salt and pepper.

Place the steak and asparagus in the baking dish and loosely cover with foil. Turn the steak after 5 minutes and leave for another 2 minutes or so. Cut the steak into thick slices and serve with the asparagus and the remaining marinade spooned over the top. Also delicious with steamed new potatoes.

Pictured on previous page

SUMMER PUDDING

160 g sugar
800 g mixed summer berries, including raspberries,
   strawberries, blueberries and redcurrants if it is
   right on Christmas
butter, for greasing
8–10 slices day-old white sandwich bread,
   crusts removed
pure thick cream or crème fraîche, to serve

Place the sugar and 2½ tablespoons water in a large saucepan over high heat and stir to dissolve the sugar. Add the berries, then turn off the heat and allow them to soften a little in the heat of the syrup.

Grease a 1 litre bowl well with butter and arrange the bread to cover completely, reserving a couple of pieces for the base of the pudding.

Spoon in the berry mixture and cover the top with the reserved bread pieces (this will become the base).

Place a saucer (just smaller in size than the top of the bowl) on the bread and add something to weigh it down, such as a tin of food. Place in the fridge overnight. Invert the pudding onto a serving plate, then cut into wedges and serve with cream or crème fraîche.

Family get-togethers (sit down)

Serves 8

We made Christmas easy and we're continuing the theme here. Minestrone is the ultimate healthy, delicious family dish and it is so simple to prepare. A couple of chooks tricked up with sage and pancetta make an easy main course served with some roast spuds or a rice salad. The chocolate pie to finish is a favourite family treat. Have a practice go for your immediate family to get the crust just right — they shouldn't be too upset about being guinea pigs for this one.

Minestrone

Roast chicken with
pancetta and sage

MINESTRONE

2 tablespoons olive oil

80 g pancetta, finely chopped

I large onion, finely chopped

3 cloves garlic, finely sliced

2 carrots, chopped or sliced

2 stalks celery, sliced

I large desiree potato, peeled and diced

⅛ white cabbage, finely shredded

10 leaves cavolo nero, washed and finely sliced crossways

¼ cup chopped flat-leaf parsley

I cup shelled green peas

10 small fresh broad beans, peeled once

I × 400 g can cannellini beans, drained and gently rinsed

about 12 basil leaves, torn

sea salt and freshly ground black pepper

extra virgin olive oil and freshly grated parmesan cheese, to serve

Italian-style bread, to serve

VEAL STOCK

400 g veal shin

I small onion, chopped

I carrot, chopped

I stalk celery, chopped

Place all the stock ingredients and 2 litres water in a large saucepan and bring to a boil, skimming off any scum that forms on top. Reduce the heat and simmer for 2 hours. Strain, discarding the solids, and set aside.

Wipe the pan clean and heat the olive oil. Cook the pancetta, onion and garlic over medium heat until the pancetta softens but doesn't brown. Add the carrot, celery, potato, cabbage, cavolo nero, parsley and stock and bring to a boil. Reduce the heat and simmer for 10 minutes, then add the peas and broad beans and simmer for another 10 minutes.

Gently stir in the cannellini beans and basil. Check the seasoning and add salt and pepper as required. Ladle into soup bowls, then drizzle with olive oil, top with grated parmesan and serve with lots of crusty Italian-style bread.

Note: I've taken the long way by making a veal stock from scratch, but if you want to save a bit of time use a good-quality bought chicken or veal stock – just make sure you water it down (the vegetables are the heroes here).

Pictured on previous page

ROAST CHICKEN WITH PANCETTA AND SAGE

2 lemons

2 organic or free-range chickens, trimmed of excess fat and patted dry with paper towel

12–14 thin slices pancetta

12–16 large sage leaves

50 g butter, melted

sea salt and freshly ground black pepper

Preheat the oven to 190°C.

Pierce the lemons a few times with a skewer and place inside each chicken, along with one slice of pancetta and a couple of sage leaves. Lay the remaining pancetta slices across the breast of each chicken to completely cover. Tuck half the sage evenly under the pancetta and lay remaining leaves on top.

Brush the legs and wings with melted butter and sprinkle on a little sea salt. Season well with pepper then place the chickens on a rack in a large roasting tin and cook for at least I hour, or until the juices run clear when the thickest part of the flesh is pierced with a sharp knife. If the juices are pink, roast for another 10 minutes.

Leave to rest for 5–10 minutes before carving.

Pictured on previous page

ITALIAN RICE SALAD

1.5 kg long-grain rice
I cup finely chopped flat-leaf parsley
I cup finely chopped basil
⅔ cup extra virgin olive oil
⅓ cup lemon juice
sea salt and freshly ground black pepper

Boil the rice in lots of salted water, stirring occasionally, until just cooked through. Drain well and rinse under cold water, then set aside to cool.

Combine the cooled rice with the remaining ingredients. Serve at room temperature, or cover and place in the fridge until ready to serve.

CHOCOLATE PIE

180 g digestive biscuits
50 g butter, plus I teaspoon extra
400 g dark chocolate (70% cocoa), broken into pieces
2 tablespoons brandy
2 tablespoons liquid glucose
600 ml pure thick cream
2 tablespoons cocoa powder

Place the biscuits in a food processor and process to a fine crumb. Melt the butter and add to the biscuit crumb to form a moist mixture. Grease a 20–25 cm pie dish with the extra butter and place the biscuit mixture in the dish, pressing gently to form a crust of even thickness.

Melt the chocolate, brandy and glucose very gently in a double boiler or in a bowl over a saucepan of barely simmering water (don't let the bottom of the bowl touch the water). Allow the mixture to cool a little.

Beat the cream in another bowl and gradually add the chocolate mixture, whisking constantly until combined. Spoon the chocolate cream into the pie case and gently smooth out the top. Cover with plastic film and chill in the refrigerator for about 2 hours. Remove from the fridge about 30 minutes before serving and dust with the cocoa.

Note: You can grease some baking paper and place it in the pie dish if you are worried about slicing and serving the base. Just lift the greaseproof paper and pie out of the dish before slicing.

Family get-togethers (stand up)

Serves 8

My wife was the marketing director of Louis Vuitton for ten years, and has run her own smarty-pants luxury-goods PR company for the past eight, so I have endured more cocktail parties, more canapés and more small talk than any bloke I know. If I never see another mini Peking duck pancake it will be too soon.

These recipes are for family affairs where there are too many people to seat (other than Gran). Simply increase the quantities to suit the size of the crowd. You can do most of the preparation in advance, and just finish them off on the night.

These aren't delicate canapés for a two-hour cocktail party – they're dishes to replace a proper seated meal. No one will go home hungry. And you can eat all of them with one hand, leaving the other free to hold a drink. Sheer genius.

Spring rolls; Seafood rolls

Italian sausage and chicken skewers with sage

Cumin and rosemary lamb cutlets

Mini galettes

SEAFOOD ROLLS

200 g prawn meat (frozen is fine)
150 g scallop meat (frozen is fine), any hard
    sinew removed
½ teaspoon pouring salt
½ teaspoon sugar
I teaspoon finely grated ginger
2 teaspoons Shaohsing rice wine
2 tablespoons chopped water chestnuts
20 frozen spring roll wrappers, thawed
neutral oil (see page 14), for pan-frying
sweet chilli sauce, soy sauce, or soy sauce mixed
    with fresh chilli, to serve

Chop the prawn and scallop meat into large pieces.
Combine the salt, sugar, ginger and rice wine in a non-
metallic bowl, add the seafood, then cover and marinate
in the fridge for an hour or two. Drain away any liquid.

Stir the water chestnuts through the seafood, then
place a spoonful of the mixture on each spring roll
wrapper and roll up tightly, tucking in the ends as you go
and dampening the edge with a little water to seal.

Heat some neutral oil in a frying pan over medium heat
and cook the seafood rolls until just golden brown. Drain
well and allow to cool just a little before serving with your
choice of dipping sauce.

Pictured on previous page

SPRING ROLLS

3 teaspoons neutral oil (see page 14)
    plus extra for pan-frying
250 g lean minced pork
3 teaspoons oyster sauce
I teaspoon soy sauce
I stalk celery, finely sliced
¼ cup chopped bamboo shoots
20 frozen spring roll wrappers, thawed
chilli or sweet chilli sauce, kecap manis, soy sauce,
    or soy sauce mixed with fresh chilli, to serve

Heat the oil in a wok or frying pan over high heat and
cook the pork, breaking up any clumps with the back of
a spoon. Add the sauces when the pork is nearly cooked.
Remove the pan from the heat and stir in the celery and
bamboo shoots (you want them to stay crunchy).

Place a spoonful of the mixture on each spring roll
wrapper and roll up tightly, tucking in the ends as you
go and dampening the edge with a little water to seal.

Heat some neutral oil in a frying pan over medium heat
and cook the spring rolls until just golden brown. Drain
well and allow to cool just a little before serving with your
choice of dipping sauce.

Pictured on previous page

ITALIAN SAUSAGE AND CHICKEN SKEWERS WITH SAGE

8 long bamboo or metal skewers
2 skinless chicken breasts, cut into 2–3 cm pieces
12 slices pancetta (not rolled), cut in half
24 large sage leaves
4 best-quality Italian pork sausages,
    cut into 2–3 cm pieces
1 large red onion, cut into 2 cm pieces
1 red capsicum, white insides and seeds removed,
    cut into 2 cm pieces
½ cup olive oil

If using bamboo skewers, soak them in water for 1 hour before use to prevent them from burning.

Wrap the chicken in the pancetta, and wrap the sage leaves around the sausage pieces. Thread the chicken, sausage, onion and capsicum alternately onto the skewers and brush with olive oil.

Chargrill or cook the skewers under the grill in your oven, turning only occasionally. Serve just as they are, or try them with soft polenta.

Pictured on previous page

CUMIN AND ROSEMARY LAMB CUTLETS

24 lamb cutlets, French trimmed
1 heaped tablespoon ground cumin
finely grated zest of 1 lemon
4 cloves garlic, finely grated or crushed
¼ cup finely chopped rosemary
½ cup olive oil
1 tablespoon sea salt, plus extra to serve
1 teaspoon freshly ground black pepper
lemon wedges, to serve

Combine all the ingredients in a bowl, then cover and marinate in the fridge for 2–4 hours.

Return the lamb to room temperature and chargrill or barbecue over very high heat until medium–rare. Sprinkle with sea salt and serve with lemon wedges.

Pictured on previous page

MINI GALETTES

butter, for greasing
6–8 sheets puff pastry, thawed
1 peach, peeled and sliced
1 punnet raspberries
½ ripe pineapple, peeled and core removed,
    thinly sliced and then quartered
1 small mango, cheeks removed and peeled,
    sliced crossways
1 granny smith apple, peeled and thinly sliced
1 organic or free-range egg, beaten
1 cup demerara sugar

Preheat the oven to 220°C and line a large baking tray with baking paper (depending on size, you may need two trays). Lightly grease the paper.

Place two pastry sheets on top of each other and cut into 4–5 cm squares or use a cutter to form 4–5 cm rounds. Repeat with the remaining pastry sheets.

Arrange the fruit in the middle of the pastries (in any combination you like) and place them on the baking tray.

Brush the pastry with beaten egg and sprinkle a little of the sugar over the fruit. Bake for 10–15 minutes until the pastry is puffed up and golden brown. Serve warm.

Pictured on previous page

Kids' birthdays

One minute it's Spiderman, then Shrek, then a monster party, then fairy tales, then Hannah Montana ('She's so last year, Dad'). In the same way, what your kids enjoy eating at birthday parties seems to change daily as they grow up.

I prefer to leave the plates of lollies, chips and kitsch cocktail frankfurts of my youth firmly in the past. These days sushi is a fave, mini meat pies from a good pie shop save heaps of time, and kids always love bowls of spaghetti. It's also fun to get kids involved with the food, especially if it is healthy, which is why the fruit or veg face-making is such a good idea.

To stop the parents swiping the kiddie food, I've included a recipe for very more-ish chicken sambos, best served with a bottle or two of chardy to calm the nerves.

I had 4–7 year olds in mind for the recipes on the following pages.

Cold pasta caprese

Orange and soy drumsticks

FRUIT FACE-MAKING COMPETITION

You can kill two birds with one stone by getting the littlies to eat something healthy and play a game at the same time.

Just grab some plastic or paper plates and a selection of fruit and vegetables that are likely to make funny faces. Kiwi fruit, bananas, anything round like blueberries – take your pick. Just give the kids plenty of options and you should have 15 minutes filled in between Pass the parcel and Pin the tail on the donkey.

COLD PASTA CAPRESE

200 g dried small penne or fettuccine
(the latter will be much messier)
iced water
12 small cherry bocconcini, each cut into
3 or 4 slices
⅔ cup Italian tomato passata
6 basil leaves, torn or shredded
⅓ cup extra virgin olive oil
sea salt and freshly ground black pepper (optional)

Cook the pasta in lots of salted boiling water until al dente. Drain and plunge into a big bowl of iced water. When cool, drain very well and mix with the remaining ingredients. Serve at room temperature.

Pictured on previous page

ORANGE AND SOY DRUMSTICKS

⅔ cup orange marmalade or jam
1 tablespoon honey
½ cup soy sauce
2 tablespoons vegetable oil
1 teaspoon finely grated ginger
12 small chicken drumsticks
1 tablespoon sesame seeds (optional)

Place all the ingredients except the chicken and sesame seeds in a small saucepan and gently stir over low heat until well combined and the marmalade or jam has melted. (You could also put the mixture in a microwave for about 20 seconds and give it a good stir.)

Transfer the mixture to a strong plastic bag, add the chicken drumsticks and rub together until the chicken is well coated. Seal the bag and refrigerate for 8–24 hours.

Preheat the oven to 190°C and line a baking tray with foil or baking paper. Place the chicken drumsticks on the tray and bake for 30 minutes until golden and cooked through. Sprinkle with sesame seeds if you like. Serve warm or cold.

Pictured on previous page

CHICKEN SAMBOS FOR THE GROWN-UPS

350 g chicken breast, trimmed of fat and sinew
2 fresh bay leaves
6 whole black peppercorns
1 stalk celery (from the middle of the bunch), finely sliced
½–⅔ cup best-quality egg mayo (preferably homemade)
2 tablespoons finely chopped flat-leaf parsley or tarragon
sea salt
12 thick slices white bread, buttered

Place the chicken, bay leaves and peppercorns in a small frying pan and add enough cold water to cover the chicken. Bring to a gentle simmer and poach for 5–10 minutes until the chicken is cooked through. Allow to cool in the liquid, then remove the chicken and finely shred with two forks.

Combine the shredded chicken, celery, mayo and parsley or tarragon. Check the seasoning and add a little salt if necessary.

Divide the mixture among the bread slices to make generous sandwiches, then trim off all the crusts and cut each sandwich into two or three fingers.

Teenage birthdays

Serves 8

Everything is starting to get complicated by now. Your daughter's friend Harry from preschool is now half a body taller than you, captain of the football team, and has broken the hearts of several ex-preschoolers. Your son's little chum Lisa is now 15, looks 23 and variously acts as if she's 35 and 12. Life wasn't meant to be easy.

So while you're battling with teenage insecurities, a houseful of hormones and checking for hidden vodka bottles, spice the food up with plenty of chilli for no other reason than it may momentarily distract them from any lustful pursuits. Oh, and good luck.

Spicy pork and pineapple kebabs;
Spicy prawn fritters

SPICY PRAWN FRITTERS

2 spring onions, very finely chopped
2 small red chillies, finely chopped
1 clove garlic, finely chopped
½ teaspoon sea salt
½ teaspoon white pepper
1 teaspoon five-spice powder
200 g plain flour
1 teaspoon baking powder
6 coriander leaves, finely chopped
1 cup iced water
neutral oil (see page 14), for deep-frying
16 green (raw) king prawns, peeled and deveined,
    tails intact
fried salt, to serve (this is simply a matter of cooking
    pouring salt in a frying pan or wok until it turns grey)
lemon wedges, to serve

Place the spring onion, chilli, garlic, salt, pepper and
five-spice in a mortar and pestle or food processor
and blend well.

Sift the flour and baking powder into a large bowl, then
add the spice mixture, coriander and iced water and mix
well. Set aside for 10 minutes.

Heat the oil in a wok or frying pan over high heat.
Dip the prawns in the batter, then deep-fry until golden
brown. Drain on paper towel.

Serve with fried salt and lemon wedges.

Pictured on previous page

SPICY MEATBALLS

4 rashers bacon, very finely chopped
2 tablespoons neutral oil (see page 14),
    plus extra for shallow-frying
1 onion, finely chopped
2 cloves garlic, crushed or finely chopped
1 red chilli, seeds removed, finely chopped
500 g premium minced pork
500 g premium minced veal
2 organic or free-range eggs, beaten
1 cup breadcrumbs made from day-old bread
    (preferably Italian)
1 teaspoon ground cumin
1 teaspoon ground oregano
1 teaspoon cayenne pepper (optional,
    if you really want to spice things up)

Cook the bacon in a frying pan until it browns. Remove
with a slotted spoon and place in a large bowl. Add oil to
the pan and cook the onion, garlic and chilli over low heat
until soft but not coloured. Allow to cool.

Add the onion mixture and remaining ingredients to
the bacon and mix very thoroughly with your hands. Roll
into bite-sized balls. Heat some neutral oil in a large frying
pan and fry the meatballs for a couple of minutes each side
until cooked through. Drain on paper towel. These can be
made ahead of time and reheated in a baking dish in the
oven. They're also pretty good cold.

SPICY PORK AND PINEAPPLE KEBABS

¼ cup hoisin sauce
2 tablespoons rice vinegar
2 tablespoons light soy sauce
2 tablespoons grated ginger
4 cloves garlic, grated or crushed
2 red chillies, very finely diced
1 kg pork neck (or leg or shoulder), cut into
    2 cm pieces
20 bamboo or metal skewers
1 pineapple, peeled and core removed,
    cut into 2 cm pieces
2 bunches spring onions, white and pale-green
    parts only, cut into 2 cm lengths

Combine the hoisin, vinegar, soy sauce, ginger, garlic and chilli in a non-metallic bowl and add the pork, turning to coat. Cover and marinate in the fridge for 4–24 hours.

If using bamboo skewers, soak them in water for 1 hour before use to prevent them from burning.

Thread a piece of pork, then pineapple, then pork then spring onion onto the skewers and brush with the remaining marinade. Barbecue over medium heat for about 10 minutes until the pork is just cooked through.

Pictured on previous page

BEEF CHILLI WITH THREE COLOURS CAPSICUM

400 g dried black-eyed peas
½ cup neutral oil (see page 14)
1 kg braising beef, very finely chopped
    (or use minced beef)
2 large onions, finely chopped
4 cloves garlic, finely chopped
2 red capsicums, white insides and
    seeds removed, cut into 1 cm dice
1 large green capsicum, white insides and
    seeds removed, cut into 1 cm dice
1 yellow capsicum, white insides and
    seeds removed, cut into 1 cm dice
2 red chillies, seeds removed, finely chopped
1 tablespoon ground cumin
3 teaspoons ground coriander
3 teaspoons ground oregano
3 teaspoons ground chilli powder
1 teaspoon smoked paprika
1 tablespoon sea salt
2 tablespoons tomato paste
4 × 400 g cans Italian diced tomatoes
2 cups beef stock
plain crackers, to serve

Soak the black-eyed peas in plenty of water for 12 hours. Drain.

Heat the oil in a large saucepan over medium heat, then add the beef and stir to stop it sticking. Add the onion and garlic and cook until soft. Add the capsicum, chilli, spices and salt and stir well to combine.

In with the tomato paste, tomato and beef stock, then add the drained black-eyed beans. If necessary, pour in enough water to just cover the ingredients.

Bring to a boil, then reduce the heat and simmer very gently, loosely covered, for 2 hours. Serve with plain crackers to crush into the chilli.

Note: This tastes even better if you make it a day or two before serving. Let it cool, then cover and store in the fridge (reheat before serving).

Nostalgia food

We all have a different view on nostalgia: drive-in movies, The Beatles at Festival Hall, mini skirts, footy grand finals on black-and-white TV, or even your first mobile phone or computer.

Like everything else, when it comes to food, it depends on when you were born. The 1970s had its dreadful apricot chicken made with canned apricots and dehydrated chicken soup. The 1980s saw an obsession with quenelles and bavarois – and more meat and fruit marriages.

My favourite bit of food nostalgia is Mum and Dad entertaining in the 1960s with the very sophisticated UDL Vodka, Lime and Soda in a can, and a tray of Jatz biscuits topped with Kraft foil-wrapped processed cheese and garish red or green pickled onions.

It is hard to believe that food has changed so much in 40 years. I wonder if my grandchildren will get a giggle out of what we think is so sophisticated today?

Classic prawn cocktail

Lamb loins 'en croute' with raspberry butter sauce

CLASSIC PRAWN COCKTAIL

¼ iceberg lettuce, finely shredded (about 2 cups)
16 large or 20 medium-sized cooked king prawns,
    peeled and deveined, tails intact if you like
freshly ground black pepper, to serve
chervil sprigs or shredded flat-leaf parsley,
    to serve (optional)
I lemon, cut into quarters, to serve
2 slices wholemeal or white bread, buttered
    and made into a sandwich, crusts removed
    and cut into quarters, to serve

MARIE ROSE SAUCE
2 organic or free-range egg yolks
¼ teaspoon pouring salt
I teaspoon Dijon mustard
180 ml olive oil
I teaspoon lemon juice
I teaspoon brandy
I heaped teaspoon tomato paste

To make the sauce, beat the egg yolks, salt and mustard
with a whisk. Add the olive oil in the slowest stream
possible, whisking constantly to make a basic mayo.
When all the oil has been incorporated and you have
a thick mayonnaise, stir in the lemon juice, brandy
and tomato paste until the sauce is an even colour.
Cover and store in the fridge until ready to serve.

Place ½ cup shredded lettuce in the bottom of four
cocktail glasses and arrange the prawns on top. Spoon
over the sauce and garnish with a grinding of pepper or
a couple of chervil sprigs or shredded parsley. Serve
with a lemon quarter and a bread-and-butter sandwich.

Pictured on previous page

CHICKEN KIEV

170 g butter, softened
4 cloves garlic, crushed
2 golden shallots, very finely chopped
2 tablespoons chopped flat-leaf parsley
2 tablespoons very finely chopped chives
4 small skinless half chicken breast fillets
I cup plain flour
sea salt and freshly ground black pepper
2 organic or free-range eggs
2 cups packaged breadcrumbs
neutral oil (see page 14), for shallow-frying
mashed potato and peas, to serve

Heat a teaspoon of the butter in a small frying pan and
soften the garlic and shallot without browning. Transfer
to a food processor, add the parsley, chives and remaining
butter and mix well (you could also place the ingredients
in a metal bowl and mash with the back of a fork). Divide
the butter mixture into four and roll up in pieces of baking
paper – you want logs about I cm wide and 3–4 cm long.
Store in the fridge until needed.

Place each chicken breast between two sheets of
baking paper and beat with a meat mallet or the bottom
of your fist until flat but with no holes. Place a log of butter
at the edge of each breast and roll into sausage-shaped
packages, folding in the ends to enclose the butter fully.

Mix together the flour, salt and pepper in a flat bowl.
Beat the eggs with a little cold water in another bowl,
and place the breadcrumbs in another.

Coat each chicken parcel with the flour. Dip in the egg,
then coat well with the breadcrumbs. Place on a plate and
refrigerate for at least 30 minutes.

Heat the oil in a deep frying pan over medium heat
(not too high – you don't want raw chicken with burnt
breadcrumbs) and cook the parcels on both sides until
golden brown. Allow to rest for a couple of minutes on
paper towel.

Sprinkle with sea salt and serve with mashed potato
and peas.

LAMB LOINS 'EN CROUTE' WITH RASPBERRY BUTTER SAUCE

2 lamb loins (the larger part of loin chops),
    trimmed of all fat and sinew
sea salt and freshly ground black pepper
1 teaspoon butter
2 sheets frozen puff pastry, thawed
4–8 English spinach leaves, stalks removed, blanched
½ teaspoon freshly grated nutmeg
4 sprigs thyme, leaves picked
1 organic or free-range egg, beaten with
    1 teaspoon water
steamed green beans and roast pumpkin, to serve

RASPBERRY BUTTER SAUCE
1 spring onion, white and pale-green part only,
    finely sliced
1 teaspoon finely grated lemon zest
¼ cup puréed raspberries
⅓ cup raspberry vinegar
200 g cold butter, diced

Preheat the oven to 220°C and line a roasting tin with baking paper.

Season the lamb with salt and pepper. Melt the butter in a frying pan and brown the lamb over high heat, without cooking through.

Place the pastry sheets on a clean work surface and trim so they are just large enough to wrap each loin. Wrap the lamb loins with the spinach and sprinkle nutmeg and thyme leaves over the top. Place the lamb on the pastry sheets and wrap so they are completely sealed.

Place the parcels, seam-side down, in the roasting tin and brush the tops with the egg wash. Bake for 10 minutes. Remove from the oven and rest for 5 minutes.

Meanwhile, make the sauce. Combine the spring onion, lemon zest, raspberry purée and vinegar in a small saucepan and simmer until reduced by half. Remove the pan from the heat and stir in the butter until melted and the sauce is smooth.

Thickly slice each lamb loin. Dollop a spoonful of sauce onto each of four plates and serve the lamb on top.

Accompany with green beans and roast pumpkin.

Pictured on previous page

CHOCOLATE MOUSSE

3 organic or free-range eggs, separated
50 g caster sugar
250 g dark chocolate (70% cocoa),
    roughly chopped
1 tablespoon brandy, Grand Marnier
    or Kahlua (optional)
300 ml thickened cream
whipped cream and strawberries or
    shaved chocolate, to serve

Beat the egg yolks and sugar in an electric mixer until pale and creamy and increased in volume.

Melt the chocolate very gently in a double boiler or in a bowl over a saucepan of barely simmering water, checking every 30 seconds (don't let the bottom of the bowl touch the water). Allow the chocolate to cool slightly, then fold in the egg and sugar mixture and liquor (if using).

Beat the cream and egg whites in separate bowls. Fold the cream through the chocolate mixture and then the egg whites. Take care with this – you want the mixture to stay light and airy.

Spoon into small glass serving bowls and refrigerate until ready to serve. Top with whipped cream and strawberries or shaved chocolate.

ACKNOWLEDGEMENTS

Three books in three years is going some.

It seems like yesterday that I started writing *The Great Aussie Barbie Cookbook*. I certainly didn't expect to write two more books within two years.

Thanks first to Julie Gibbs, the head honcho at Penguin in Sydney, who had the faith to commission the second and third books even before the previous titles had time to prove themselves.

The Penguin team of managing editor Ingrid Ohlsson, designer Daniel New and editor Virginia Birch has been a dream to work with over the past three years. Things are very easy when you know you'll be delivered such a high level of professionalism. I must acknowledge the great job done by Sally Bateman, who heads up the publicity department, and Kim Noble, who has looked after each of the books. Thanks also to editors Rachel Carter and Ariane Durkin.

We managed to keep the same team for all three books, just changing between some of Australia's very best food stylists each time. For this book, it was Michelle Noerianto's turn and she did a fabulous job. She also had the easiest (and funniest) working relationship with photographer Rob Palmer, whose work has really provided us with an edge in the cluttered cookbook market.

Part of the reason that the food looks so good on the page is simply that it is such good produce. AC Butchery, Fratelli Fresh, Steve Costi Seafoods and Christie's, take a bow: all trusted suppliers who make great produce accessible to everyone, not just the food industry. Special thanks to Mao & More: (02) 9699 2700, Rickrack Retro: (02) 9798 8401 and Major & Tom: (02) 9557 8380 for the props.

Finally, thanks to family and friends who appeared as talent in the photos, including my daughter Zoe, cousin Sophie, my old man, Cookie the wonder dog, Caleb, Claudia, Maisie, Marcus, Oliver, Stella, Harry, Tristan and Zai. And to my long-suffering wife Naomi and her parents who, with Zoe, made up the Tuesday-night tasting panel as I tested the recipes (sometimes up to half a dozen at a time).

It feels like the end of a James Bond movie. But keep an eye out for the next *Great Aussie* production, coming soon to all good bookshops . . .

INDEX

VIKING

Published by the Penguin Group
Penguin Group (Australia)
250 Camberwell Road, Camberwell, Victoria 3124, Australia
(a division of Pearson Australia Group Pty Ltd)
Penguin Group (USA) Inc.
375 Hudson Street, New York, New York 10014, USA
Penguin Group (Canada)
90 Eglinton Avenue East, Suite 700, Toronto, ON M4P 2Y3, Canada
(a division of Pearson Penguin Canada Inc.)
Penguin Books Ltd
80 Strand, London WC2R 0RL, England
Penguin Ireland
25 St Stephen's Green, Dublin 2, Ireland
(a division of Penguin Books Ltd)
Penguin Books India Pvt Ltd
11 Community Centre, Panchsheel Park, New Delhi 110 017, India
Penguin Group (NZ)
67 Apollo Drive, Rosedale, North Shore 0632, New Zealand
(a division of Pearson New Zealand Ltd)
Penguin Books (South Africa) (Pty) Ltd
24 Sturdee Avenue, Rosebank, Johannesburg 2196, South Africa

Penguin Books Ltd, Registered Offices: 80 Strand, London, WC2R 0RL, England

First published by Penguin Group (Australia), 2010

10 9 8 7 6 5 4 3 2 1

Design by Daniel New © Penguin Group (Australia)
Photography by Rob Palmer
Styling by Michelle Noerianto
Typeset in Gill Sans by Post Pre-press Group, Brisbane, Queensland
Colour reproduction by Splitting Image Colour Studio Pty Ltd, Clayton, Victoria
Printed in China by Everbest Printing Co. Ltd.

National Library of Australia
Cataloguing-in-Publication data:

Terakes, Kim.
The great Aussie bloke's cookbook / Kim Terakes
9780670073429 (pbk.)
Includes index.
Cookery, Australian

641.5994

penguin.com.au